BREAKING CURSES DELIVERANCE MANUAL

By Gene Moody

Deliverance Ministries
Gene B. Moody
14930 Jefferson Highway
Baton Rouge, LA 70817-5217
www.genemoody.com

Telephone: (225) 755-8870
Fax: (225) 755-6120

NOT COPYRIGHTED
This manual is not copyrighted
I encourage you to make copies and distribute them for the Glory of God.
You may freely use the lessons as God directs you!

BREAKING CURSES DELIVERANCE MANUAL

TABLE OF CONTENTS - OVERVIEW

SECTION 1 – SUMMARY REVIEW OF CURSES 1

SECTION 2 - BIBLICAL CURSES 5

SECTION 3 PRAYERS AND LISTS OF CURSE DEMONS 19

SECTION 4 - WORD CURSES 43

SECTION 5 - CURSING OTHERS AND BEING CURSED 58

SECTION 6 - HOUSE CURSES 68

SECTION 8 - FEMALE CURSES 84

SECTION 9 - CURSES OF APOSTATE CHURCH 86

SECTION 11 - CURSES FOR SHEDDING INNOCENT BLOOD 96

SECTION 12 - INCEST AND BASTARD CURSES 104

SECTION 13 - BREAKING THE CURSE OFF BLACK AMERICA 111

SECTION 14 - CURSE OF AHAB AND JEZEBEL 115

SECTION 15 - CURSES OF THE SERPENT 131

SECTION 16 – DELIVERANCE AMONG AFRICAN-AMERICANS 133

SECTION 17 - AFRICAN AMERICAN DEMONS 135

SECTION 19 - AMERICAN INDIAN CURSES 143

SECTION 20 - ALASKAN NATIVE CURSES 153

BREAKING CURSES DELIVERANCE MANUAL

TABLE OF CONTENTS – DETAILED

SECTION 1 – SUMMARY REVIEW OF CURSES 1
   BIBLICAL CURSES 1
      Preface 1
      All Curses 1
      Of Curses 2
      God 2
      Nationality And Language 2
      Bloodline 2
      Others Outside of the Bloodline 2
      Ourselves (or Ancestors) 2
   CURSES ON CHILDREN 2
   THE CURSE OF AHAB AND JEZEBEL 2
   THE INCEST AND BASTARD CURSES 3
   CURSES FOR SHEDDING INNOCENT BLOOD 3
   INDIAN CURSES 3
   ARE YOU LIVING WITH A CURSE? 4
   CURSING OTHERS AND BEING CURSED 4
   SIX STEPS TO FREEDOM FROM CURSES 4

SECTION 2 - BIBLICAL CURSES 5
   LIST OF SCRIPTURE 5
   HOW DID WE LEARN ABOUT CURSES? 6
   HOW DO CURSES TAKE EFFECT? 6
   SCRIPTURE ABOUT THE CURSE OF THE BASTARD AND INCEST 6
   OBSERVATIONS ABOUT BASTARDS 6
   HOW ARE CURSES IDENTIFIED? 7
   THE CURSE OF AHAB AND JEZEBEL BOOKLETS 7
   AHAB / JEZEBEL CURSES FOUND IN THE BIBLE 7
   AHAB/JEZEBEL REBELLIOUS INFLUENCE IN THE WORLD 7
   GENE'S AHAB CHARACTERISTICS 7
   HOW ARE CURSES RECOGNIZED THAT COME FROM ANCESTORS? 8
   BLESSINGS AND CURSES 8
   EARLINE'S TESTIMONY ABOUT HER ANCESTRAL BACKGROUND 8
   HOW ARE CURSES BROKEN? 9
   WHAT IS DONE AFTER THE CURSE IS BROKEN? 9
   RESULTS OF BREAKING CURSES 9
   STEPS TO FREEDOM FROM CURSES 9
   CURSED OBJECTS ON YOU AND IN YOUR HOME 9
   FIVE STEPS TO CLEANING HOUSE OF CURSED OBJECTS 10
   SUMMARY 10
   BLESSINGS, CURSES AND DURATION 10
   BIBLICAL CURSES (EXCERPTS) 11
   CURSES ON CHILDREN 13

- A CURSE AGAINST PROTESTANTS (EXCERPTS) 13
- CURSES (EXCERPTS) 13
- VOWS AND CURSES (EXCERPTS) 15
- HEX SIGNS (EXCERPTS) 15
- SYMBOLS OF HEX SIGNS (EXCERPTS) 16
- BREAKING CURSES 16
- DEMONS SENT BY BIBLICAL CURSES 17
- REFERENCES 18

SECTION 3 PRAYERS AND LISTS OF CURSE DEMONS 19
- OVERALL PRAYER 20
- OVERALL COMMANDS 20
- WORD CURSES 20
  - Christian Fantasy Prayer 20
  - Lies, Deceit And Flattery Prayer 20
- LIST OF DEMONS 21
  - Christian Fantasy - Lies Not Truth 21
  - Lies, Deceit And Flattery 21
  - Bad Habits Of Thinking And Reacting 21
- BIBLICAL CURSES 21
  - Prayer 21
  - List Of Demons 22
  - Prayer 23
  - List Of Demons 23
- ALASKAN NATIVE CURSES 26
  - Prayer To Break Curses 26
  - Prayer 26
  - List Of Demons 27
- AFRICAN AMERICAN CURSES 27
  - Breaking The Willie Lynch Curse Prayer 27
  - Deliverance 27
- WALLS OF ARGUMENT PRAYER 28
  - Deliverance 28
  - List Of Demons 28
  - Sins / Curses / Demons 28
  - Various Demons 28
  - Sex 28
  - Infirmity 29
  - Death 29
  - Religion 29
  - Addictions 29
  - Slavery 29
  - Black Interaction 29
  - Occult 29
  - Black 30
  - Demonic Tongues 30
  - Matriarchal 30
- CURSING OTHERS AND BEING CURSED 30

- Prayer 30
- List Of Demons 30
- ARE YOU LIVING WITH A CURSE? 31
  - Commands 31
- CURSES FOR SHEDDING INNOCENT BLOOD 31
  - Prayer 31
  - List Of Demons 32
- HOUSE CURSES 32
  - Cleaning Your House Prayer 32
- CURSE OF PRIDE 32
  - Prayer 32
  - List Of Demons 33
- CURSE OF AHAB AND JEZEBEL 33
  - Prayer 33
  - Ahab And Jezebel Demons Short List 34
  - Ahab And Jezebel Demons Long List 36
  - Ahab Demons 36
  - Jezebel Demons 38

SECTION 4 - WORD CURSES 43
OVERALL CURSES 45
- Scripture 45
- Scripture For Victorious Living 46
- Preface 47
- Are You Living With A Curse? 47
- All Curses 47
- Sources Of Curses 47
  - God 47
- Ourselves 47
- Six Steps To Freedom From Curses 47
- Curses On Children 48
- Prayer For Biblical Curses 48
CLEANING YOUR HOUSE 48
- Five Steps 48
- Prayer 48
CURSING OTHERS AND BEING CURSED 49
- Spoken Curses 49
- Ancestral Curses 49
- Parental Curses 49
- Cursing By People Other Than Your Ancestors 49
- Cursing Yourself 49
- Origin Of Curses 49
- The Curse Of Charismatic Witchcraft 50
- Prayer 50
PSYCHIC PRAYERS 50
- Testimony 50
CHRISTIAN FANTASY 51
- Preface 51

- Definitions 51
- Lies 51
- Christian Fables And Cliches 52
  - Untruths 52
  - Truths 52
- Prophecy Myths 52
- General Myths 53
- Prayer Before Deliverance 53
- LIES, DECEIT AND FLATTERY 53
  - The Little White Lie 53
  - Evangelistically Speaking 54
  - The Deliberate Lie 54
  - Flattery 54
  - Pretending 54
  - Deceit And Deception 55
  - Falseness 55
  - Cheating 55
  - Dishonesty 55
  - Responsibility Of A Minister 55
  - Prayer 55
  - List Of Demons 56
    - Christian Fantasy - Lies Not Truth 56
    - Lies, Deceit And Flattery 56
    - Bad Habits Of Thinking And Reacting 56

SECTION 5 - CURSING OTHERS AND BEING CURSED 58
- COMMENTS 58
- SOME THOUGHTS 58
- BLESSING OTHERS AND BEING BLESSED 59
- PSYCHIC PRAYERS 60
- SPOKEN CURSES 60
- ANCESTRAL CURSES 60
- PARENTAL CURSES 61
- CURSING BY OTHERS OTHER THAN YOUR ANCESTORS 61
- CURSING YOURSELF 61
- CURSING YOUR DESCENDENTS 62
- ORIGIN OF CURSES 62
- BIBLICAL CURSES 62
- THE CURSE OF DISOBEDIENCE 62
- THE CURSE OF AHAB AND JEZEBEL (BOOKLETS) 63
- THE CURSE OF CHARISMATIC WITCHCRAFT 63
- THE CURSE OF THE BASTARD (BOOKLET) 63
- THE INDIAN CURSES 63
- CURSED OBJECTS 64
- SUMMARY 64
- SPIRITUAL WARFARE 64
- LIST OF DEMONS 66

SECTION 6 - HOUSE CURSES 68
SCRIPTURES 68
TESTIMONIES 69
Seven-Month Old Child 69
Marie Moody 69
Asian People 69
SHOULD HOUSES BE CLEANSED OF EVIL SPIRITS? (EXCERPTS) 69
NOTES ON WITCHCRAFT, SYMBOLS AND ACCURSED OBJECTS (EXCERPTS) 70
CURSED OBJECTS AND POSSESSIONS 71
Cursed Objects (Excerpts) 71
A Word About Incense (Excerpts) 71
Cursed Objects And Demon Infestation (Excerpts) 71
Cursed And Inanimate Objects 72
SIGNS AND SYMBOLS 73
Hex Signs (Excerpts) 73
Symbols Of Hex Signs (Excerpts) 73
Masonic Symbols (Excerpts) 74
Symbols 74
TOYS 75
Dolls (Excerpts) 75
Dolls In Toledo, Ohio (Excerpts) 75
Baby - Seven Months Old (Excerpts) 75
Satan In The Toy Store 76
Toys Having Either Occult Linkage, Actions Or Excessive Violence 77
CLEANING YOUR HOUSE OF DEMONIC OBJECTS 78
To Exorcise Inanimate Objects (Excerpts) 78
Five Steps To Cleaning House 79
PRAYER 80
REFERENCES 80
EZEKIEL 8:5-18 81
King James Version 81
Amplified Version 81
IDOLATRY 82
PUNISHMENT 82
COMMENTS 83
REFERENCE 83

SECTION 8 - FEMALE CURSES 84
ISAIAH 3:16-26 84
King James Version 84
Amplified Version 84
ANALYSIS OF SCRIPTURE 85
COMMENTS 85
MINISTRY 85

SECTION 9 - CURSES OF APOSTATE CHURCH 86
WHAT IS THE APOSTATE CHURCH? 86
A UNITED METHODIST CHURCH 87

- IT IS ABOUT SELF! 87
- WHAT IS SEXUAL SIN? 87
- WHAT IS SIN? 88
- REFERENCE 88
- SCRIPTURES 89
  - Pride Scriptures 89
  - Other Pride Scriptures 90
  - Proud Scriptures 90
  - Other Proud Scriptures 91
  - Proudly Scriptures 91
  - Other Proudly Scriptures 91
  - Humble Scriptures 91
  - Other Humble Scriptures 92
- SPIRITUAL 92
- EXAMPLES 93
- PROBLEMS 93
- PRAYER 93
- LIST OF DEMONS 94
- GOD HATES PRIDE 94
- PRAYER OF REPENTANCE FROM PRIDE 95

SECTION 11 - CURSES FOR SHEDDING INNOCENT BLOOD 96
- PREFACE 96
- CAIN AND ABLE 97
- MANASSEH 98
- AHAB AND JEZEBEL 98
- AS A CHILD 99
- TAKING A BRIBE 99
- JESUS' CONDEMNATION 100
- CHILD SACRIFICE 100
- INNOCENT BLOOD 101
- GENE'S COMMENTS 102
- PRAYER 103
- LIST OF DEMONS 103

SECTION 12 - INCEST AND BASTARD CURSES 104
- PREFACE 104
- HE CURSE OF INCEST 104
  - Scripture 104
  - Incest And Bastards In The Church 104
  - Comments 105
  - Earline's Comments As A Teacher 105
- THE CURSE OF THE BASTARD 106
  - Scripture 106
  - Observations About Bastards 106
  - Sex Diseases And Crimes 107
  - Examples 107
    - Four Family Generations 107

- Unsaved to Saved 108
- The Curse of the Bastard in Earline's Life 108
- King David 108
- Youth And Adults 109
  - Young People 109
  - Adults 109
- Curse Of The Bastard Bondage 109
- Abnormal Sexual Behavior In Pagan Worship 109
- Repentance And Forgiveness 109
  - REFERENCES 110

SECTION 13 - BREAKING THE CURSE OFF BLACK AMERICA 111
- REFERENCE 114

SECTION 14 - CURSE OF AHAB AND JEZEBEL 115
- LIST OF SCRIPTURE ABOUT AHAB, JEZEBEL AND OTHERS 115
  - Scripture 115
  - Other Families In The Bible 115
  - Ahab 116
- CURSES FOUND IN THE BIBLE 116
- TESTIMONIES ABOUT AHAB AND JEZEBEL 117
- AHAB / JEZEBEL 117
- RESULTS OF AHAB / JEZEBEL RELATIONSHIP 117
- AHAB / JEZEBEL REBELLIOUS INFLUENCE IN THE WORLD 117
- EFFECT ON CHILDREN OF AHAB / JEZEBEL 118
- YOU AND PEOPLE AROUND YOU 118
- CURSE OF AHAB - SCRIPTURE EXPLANATION 118
- AHAB CHARACTERISTICS 119
- GENE'S AHAB CHARACTERISTICS 120
- AHAB REBELS 120
- JEZEBEL REBELS 120
- ELIJAH DESTROYS BAAL'S PROPHETS (I KINGS 18:17-40) 121
- PRAYER 121
- AHAB AND JEZEBEL DEMONS 122
  - Ahab Demons 122
- AHAB AND JEZEBEL DEMONS 124
- REFERENCES 130

SECTION 15 - CURSES OF THE SERPENT 131
- TREAD ON SERPENTS 131
- CORRUPTING BEGUILING SUBTLE SERPENT 131
- FIERY SERPENT WORSHIP 131
- SERPENT TONGUES 131
- SERPENT BITES 132
- PIERCING CROOKED DRAGON SERPENT 132
- DRAGON DEVIL SATAN SERPENT 132
- COMMENTS 132

SECTION 16 – DELIVERANCE AMONG AFRICAN-AMERICANS	133
SECTION 17 - AFRICAN AMERICAN DEMONS	135
SINS / CURSES / DEMONS	135
LISTS OF DEMONS	135
SEX	136
INFIRMITY	136
DEATH	136
RELIGION	136
ADDICTIONS	136
SLAVERY	136
BLACK INTERACTION	136
Occult	136
Black	137
Demonic tongues	137
Matriarchal	137
CONTENTS	138
PREFACE	138
RELATIONSHIPS	138
MORALITY AND CHARACTER	138
RELIGION	138
Prayer	138
Deliverance	138
RELIGIOUS SPIRITS	138
Control Spirits	138
False Spirits	138
Witchcraft And Voodoo Spirits	138
LIST OF DEMONS	138
Various Demons	138
Sex	138
Infirmity	138
Death	138
Religion	138
Addictions	138
Slavery	138
Black Interaction	138
Occult	138
Black	138
Demonic Tongues	138
Matriarchal	138
REFERENCES	138
PREFACE	138
RELATIONSHIPS	138
MORALITY AND CHARACTER	138
RELIGION	139
Prayer	139
Deliverance	139
RELIGIOUS SPIRITS	139

- Control Spirits 139
- False Spirits 139
- Witchcraft And Voodoo Spirits 139
- LIST OF DEMONS 139
  - Various Demons 140
  - Sex 140
  - Infirmity 140
  - Death 140
  - Religion 140
  - Addictions 141
  - Slavery 141
  - Black Interaction 141
  - Occult 141
  - Black 141
  - Demonic Tongues 141
  - Matriarchal 141
- REFERENCES 141

SECTION 19 - AMERICAN INDIAN CURSES 143
- SCRIPTURES 143
- AMERICA IS A MELTING POT 143
- EARLINE'S TESTIMONY ABOUT HER HEART CONDITION 143
  - Earline 143
  - Gene 144
  - Earline 144
  - Gene 144
  - Earline 144
  - Gene 144
- INDIAN CURSES (EXCERPTS) 145
- DELIVERANCE OF AN EAGLE SCOUT (EXCERPTS) 146
- PRAYER 149
- LIST OF DEMONS 150

SECTION 20 - ALASKAN NATIVE CURSES 153
- PREFACE 153
- SOCIAL ORGANIZATION 154
  - Gender Roles 154
  - Marriage 154
- RELIGIONS 154
- BELIEFS 155
  - Unangan 155
  - Aleut 155
  - Koniag Alutiiq 155
  - Central Yup'ik 155
  - Inupiat 155
  - Athabaskan 156
  - Tlingit And Haida 156
- KNOWLEDGE SPECIALISTS 156

  Shaman Battle 157
SPIRITUAL CEREMONIES AND RITUALS 157
  Menstrual Period 157
  Slaves 157
CEREMONIAL PARAPHERNALIA 158
OBJECTS 158
ADORNMENT 158
  Tattoos 158
WHALING 158
  Hunter's Wife 159
HUNTING AND FISHING 159
WARFARE AND PEACE 160
DWELLINGS 160
BOATS 160
TOTEM POLES 160
MUMMIES 160
HISTORIC CHANGE 160
FUTURE 161
PRAYER 161
BASIC DELIVERANCE 162
LIST OF SPIRITS 162
REFERENCES 162

SECTION 1 – SUMMARY REVIEW OF CURSES

CONTENTS
1. **BIBLICAL CURSES**
   1. PREFACE
   2. ALL CURSES
   3. SOURCES OF CURSES
      1. God
      2. Bloodline
      3. Others Outside of the Bloodline
      4. Ourselves (or Ancestors)
2. **CURSES ON CHILDREN**
3. **THE CURSE OF AHAB AND JEZEBEL**
4. **THE INCEST AND BASTARD CURSES**
5. **CURSES FOR SHEDDING INNOCENT BLOOD**
6. **INDIAN CURSES**
7. **ARE YOU LIVING WITH A CURSE?**
8. **CURSING OTHERS AND BEING CURSED**
9. **SIX STEPS TO FREEDOM FROM CURSES**

BIBLICAL CURSES
Preface

This lesson will look at curses overall and cover a lot of areas where we can receive curses. The effects can be many in our spirit, soul and body. You could say in our spiritual, mental, physical and material lives, i.e. everything that affects us. This includes our nation, ancestors, ourselves, descendents, and others, or anyone or anything that can affect us.
*

For instance, curses cause poverty, need and want. The love of money is the root of all evil and leads to many curses. **Sex, power, and money are three main destroyers of man. If you let any of these control you, it will destroy you.**

All Curses

Deut. 28:15 **But it shall come to pass, if thou wilt not hearken unto the voice of the Lord thy God, to observe to do all His commandments and His statutes which I command thee this day; that all these curses shall come upon thee, and overtake thee.**

For every verse in THE HOLY BIBLE that you obey, you are blessed. For every verse in THE HOLY BIBLE that you disobey, you are cursed. You can read the Scripture and see the curses and consequences of disobeying the commandments and statutes. We are told to keep all the words of the Holy Bible. GOD is serious about us obeying His inspired WORD OF GOD.

Of Curses
There are many sources of curses. Basically overall there are five main sources of curses: our nationality, bloodline, others, GOD and ourselves.

God
The main source of curses is disobeying THE BIBLE.

Nationality And Language
1. The sins of our **nation** as a whole and the particular part of the **land** that we live in.
2. Our **nationality** including language, race, culture, creed and whatever would pertain to it.

Bloodline
1. The **ancestors and descendents.**

Others Outside of the Bloodline
1. Those who have **spiritual authority** over us such as husbands over wives, parents over children, spiritual leaders over those led, teachers over those taught.
2. Those that **abuse** us: mentally, physically, spiritually and financially.

Ourselves (or Ancestors)
1. Having **cursed objects** in our home or possessions.
2. **Ourselves** when we curse others.
3. **Shedding innocent blood** such as abortion.
4. **Out of divine order** with GOD.
5. **Creating bastards and have incest** or hurt GOD's creation through sexual sins.

CURSES ON CHILDREN
1. Children born from incestuous unions (Gen. 19:36-38).
2. Curse of idol worship extends to **fourth generation** of great grandchildren (Exodus 20:1-5).
3. Children who strike their parents (Exodus 21:15).
4. Those who curse their parents (Exodus 21:17).
5. Iniquity of fathers on children (Exodus 34:6-7).
6. Children wandered for forty years in the desert (Numbers 14:18 & 33).
7. Idol worship (Deut. 5:9-10).
8. Rebellious children (Deut. 21:18-21).
9. Curse of the bastard extends to **tenth generation** of descendants (Deut. 23:2).
10. In son's days evil will come on his house (I Kings 21:19).
11. The iniquity of the father upon the children (Jer. 32:18).

THE CURSE OF AHAB AND JEZEBEL
Isaiah 3:12 **As for my people, children are their oppressors, and women rule over them. O my people, they which lead thee cause thee to err, and destroy the way of thy paths.**

The man cannot escape his responsibility by blaming his problems on the woman. Finally, children are open to satanic attack and will usually become like their parents! Some women and men today use seemingly pure religious motives to control others such as prophecy - telling others what to do; soulish prophecy is charismatic witchcraft.

THE INCEST AND BASTARD CURSES

If anyone of your ten-generations of 2048 ancestors created a bastard or participated in incest, you are cursed. One family affected 1200 people in six generations. Incest can especially lead to women hating all men. As we engage in these sexual acts, GOD told Earline we are worshiping Satan.

Deut. 23:2 **A bastard shall not enter into the congregation of the Lord; even to his tenth generation shall he not enter into the congregation of the Lord.**

Deuteronomy 23:3 **An Ammonite or Moabite shall not enter into the congregation of the LORD; even to their tenth generation shall they not enter into the congregation of the LORD forever (incest).**

I Cor. 6:18 **Flee fornication. Every sin that a man doeth is without the body; but he that committeth fornication sinneth against his own body.**

Here is something to consider: God has issued a three to four generation curse against the family line of those who worship other God's, but He has issued a curse for ten generations on those who conceive bastards or practice incest. God is more concerned about what we do to hurt our offspring than about worship of other Gods.

People with the bastard curse on them have trouble with religious deception. They cause trouble and strife in churches and groups.

CURSES FOR SHEDDING INNOCENT BLOOD

Psa. 106:36-38 **And served their idols, which were a snare to them. Yes,, they sacrificed their sons and their daughters to demons, And shed innocent blood, even the blood of their sons and their daughters, whom they sacrificed to the idols of Canaan; and the land was polluted with blood.**

INDIAN CURSES

Leviticus 26:40-41 If they shall confess their iniquity, and the iniquity of their father, with their trespass which they trespassed against me, and that also they have walked contrary unto me; And that I also have walked contrary unto them, and have brought them into the land of their enemies; if then their uncircumcised hearts be humbled, and they then accept of the punishment of their iniquity.

Exodus 20:3-5 Thou shalt have no other Gods before me. Thou shalt not make unto thee any graven image, or any likeness of anything that is in heaven above, or that is in the earth beneath, or that is in the water under the earth: Thou shalt not bow down thyself to them, nor serve them: for I the LORD thy God am a jealous God, visiting the iniquity of the fathers upon the children unto the third and fourth generation of them that hate me. Repent for your ancestors and yourself for the sin of idol worship. The curse of idol worship follows the blood line.

ARE YOU LIVING WITH A CURSE?
<u>A curse has been defined as: uttering a wish of evil against one; to imprecate evil; to call for mischief or injury to fall upon; to execrate, to bring evil upon or to; to blast, vex, harass or torment with great calamities.</u>

What The Church needs more than anything else is deliverance. They will never win the battle with Satan without deliverance.

CURSING OTHERS AND BEING CURSED
Ministers and Christian Leaders should think about standing before God and explaining why you did not teach certain areas of the Bible. Can you see that the minister is doing his congregation a disservice? This is frightening when you think about the consequences of your actions on your children.

Deut. 5:7-9 Thou shalt have none other Gods before me. Thou shalt not make thee any graven image, or any likeness of any thing that is in heaven above, or that is in the earth beneath, or that is in the waters beneath the earth: Thou shalt not bow down thyself unto them, nor serve them: for I the Lord thy God am a jealous God, visiting the iniquity of the fathers upon the children unto the third and fourth generation of them that hate me.
Deut. 7:26 Neither shalt thou bring an abomination into thine house lest thou be a cursed thing like it; but thou shalt utterly abhor it for it is a cursed thing.
Deut. 28:1-2 And it shall come to pass, if thou shalt (shalt not) hearken diligently unto the voice of the Lord thy God, to observe and to do all his commandments which I command thee this day, that the Lord thy God will set (not set) thee on high above all nations of the earth: and all these blessings shall (shall not) come on thee, and overtake thee, if thou shalt (shalt not) hearken unto the voice of the Lord thy God.
Prov. 26:2 As the bird by wandering, as the swallow by flying, so the curse causeless shall not come.
Ecc. 10:20 Curse not the king, no not in thy thought; and curse not the rich in thy bedchamber: for a bird of the air (probably a demon) shall carry the voice, and that which hath wings shall tell the matter.
I Tim. 6:10 For the love of money is the root of all evil: which while some coveted after, they have erred from the faith, and pierced themselves through with many sorrows.

SIX STEPS TO FREEDOM FROM CURSES
1. **Identify the name** of the curse and the sin that caused the curse.
2. **Forgive** those that caused the curses for their sin against you in placing this curse on the family line.
3. **Repent and pray** to God to take away the right for the curses to be in our lives.
4. **Break the curse** in the Name of Jesus Christ.
5. **Cast out the demons** that came in with the curse.
6. **Discipline your life** and sin no more.

SECTION 2 - BIBLICAL CURSES

CONTENTS
1. LIST OF SCRIPTURE
2. HOW DID WE LEARN ABOUT CURSES?
3. HOW DO CURSES TAKE EFFECT?
4. SCRIPTURE ABOUT THE CURSE OF THE BASTARD AND INCEST
5. OBSERVATIONS ABOUT BASTARDS
6. HOW ARE CURSES IDENTIFIED?
7. THE CURSE OF AHAB AND JEZEBEL BOOKLETS
8. AHAB / JEZEBEL CURSES FOUND IN THE BIBLE
9. AHAB/JEZEBEL REBELLIOUS INFLUENCE IN THE WORLD
10. GENE'S AHAB CHARACTERISTICS
11. HOW ARE CURSES RECOGNIZED THAT COME FROM ANCESTORS?
12. BLESSINGS AND CURSES
13. EARLINE'S TESTIMONY ABOUT HER ANCESTRAL BACKGROUND
14. HOW ARE CURSES BROKEN?
15. WHAT IS DONE AFTER THE CURSE IS BROKEN?
16. RESULTS OF BREAKING CURSES
17. STEPS TO FREEDOM FROM CURSES
18. CURSED OBJECTS ON YOU AND IN YOUR HOME
19. FIVE STEPS TO CLEANING HOUSE OF CURSED OBJECTS
20. SUMMARY
21. BLESSINGS, CURSES AND DURATION
22. BIBLICAL CURSES
23. CURSES ON CHILDREN
24. A CURSE AGAINST PROTESTANTS
25. CURSES
26. VOWS AND CURSES
27. HEX SIGNS
28. SYMBOLS OF HEX SIGNS
29. BREAKING CURSES
30. DEMONS SENT BY BIBLICAL CURSES
31. REFERENCES

LIST OF SCRIPTURE

Exodus 34:6-7 Iniquity of fathers on the children.
Num. 14:18, 33 Children wandered for 40 years.
Deut. 5:9-10 Idol worship.
Joshua 24:19-20 Serving strange Gods.
I Kings 21:29 In son's days, evil will come on his house.
Job 10:14 Visiting mine iniquity.
Psalms 79:8 Remember not against us former iniquities.
Isaiah 64:9 Neither remember iniquity forever.
Jer. 32:18 The iniquity of the father upon the children.

Micah 6:11 Wicked balances.
Nahum 1:3 Will not acquit the wicked.

HOW DID WE LEARN ABOUT CURSES?

We learned through twelve years of intensive experience of working with thousands of people. We learned in mass deliverance with groups of people and especially in ministry to individuals. We learned by spending sufficient hours with individuals to find out what was wrong with them and then taking the time to get rid of demons that were holding on. The ministry to others is a proving ground for the knowledge we have gained. After twelve years, we are constantly learning more about how the enemy operates; you never learn it all!

Our ministry changed dramatically when we learned that we needed to break curses and how to do it. Our deliverance sessions became more smooth with less manifestations and violence. It is as simple as this; if the demons have a right to remain before God because of a curse, you will not be able to cast them out or, if you do, they will be able to come back and re-enter the person.

I am a trained engineer; I am trained to learn how things work. I want to figure out how the Kingdom of God works. I teach you what I have learned; I intend to keep learning until I die. The Bible is like an engineer's handbook. **God told me to accept the Bible in simple childlike faith, put it into practice and watch it work!**

HOW DO CURSES TAKE EFFECT?

Curses take effect when you or your ancestors have committed certain acts which are contrary to the Word of God. This is an act of sin which then brings curses on you and your descendents. The demons will then try to perpetuate the curse for all remaining generations of descendents. The demons can enter the child in the womb at conception. The child enters life with this characteristic which is demonic. The world would say that the child inherited this characteristic from his ancestors. What was inherited was a demon passed down through the blood line.

SCRIPTURE ABOUT THE CURSE OF THE BASTARD AND INCEST

A person begotten out of wedlock shall not enter into the assembly of the Lord; even until his tenth generation shall his descendants not enter into the congregation of the Lord (Deut. 23:2).

OBSERVATIONS ABOUT BASTARDS

When a bastard is conceived in lust, it is not true love. True love is protecting and providing. Neither is present when the bastard is conceived. Demons of lust will follow all children of this line. Besides lust, all types of demons follow them and try to gain entrance.

Present day observations include more bastards, family and personal rebellion, sickness, suicide, can't feel welcome or at peace in God's house, murder, delinquency and mental illness.

HOW ARE CURSES IDENTIFIED?

We learned to recognize many curses by name either through experience, or by the names or characteristics mentioned in the Bible. Sometimes we break curses because the demon says it has a right to remain because of the curse; this happens many times when a demon will not leave. Sometimes we break curses because we feel impressed by the Holy Spirit to do so. Nothing is lost by breaking a curse that does not exist; everything is gained by breaking a curse that does exist.

THE CURSE OF AHAB AND JEZEBEL BOOKLETS

Two excellent booklets have been printed by the Hegewisch Baptist Church: **The Curse of Ahab** for men and **The Curse of Jezebel** for women. Each person will receive a copy - Men: **Ahab** and women: **Jezebel**. Men may also have Jezebelic tendencies; women - Ahab tendencies:

AHAB / JEZEBEL CURSES FOUND IN THE BIBLE

The relationship of Ahab and Jezebel provides an excellent illustration of the curse brought about by a husband and wife being out of God's divine order for the family. This curse can be traced back all the way to Adam and Eve. It can be found through the Bible being manifested in different families.

God puts the greatest burden of responsibility on the men, not the women. If the men were not Ahabs and were, in fact, priests and heads of their homes, then the women would not be Jezebels! **The man cannot escape his responsibility by blaming his problems on the woman.**

AHAB/JEZEBEL REBELLIOUS INFLUENCE IN THE WORLD

1. Divorce - one parent families.
2. Felinism - pictures bungling father and clever mother.
3. Sex - no restrictions.
4. Young people - confused, rebellious.
5. Drugs - Sex - Music.
6. Society with emotional problems.
7. Effeminate, emotional, weak spiritual and weak physical men.
8. Women's false strength - put to test usually fails.

GENE'S AHAB CHARACTERISTICS

1. Leaving spiritual leadership up to Earline about how to raise our children.
2. Breakdown of communications between Earline, Marie and me as I pursued spiritual goals but neglected my family.
3. Fear of getting hurt by others especially by my family and Earline's family.
4. God of Jobs at one time when I put my job first, family second and God last. Now it is reversed: God first, family second and job last.
5. Leaving spiritual things of God to wife occurred partially such as receiving the Baptism. I suggested that Earline receive it first.
6. I came from a poor family and had a materialistic drive until Byron died.

7. We had many misunderstandings as Ahab husband and Jezebel wife.
8. I did not believe in having an argument with my wife. So, I would go into my room, study engineering, and not talk to Earline.
9. We even came close to separation and divorce at our low point about twenty-five years ago after Byron died.
10. I was somewhat unemotional and could not show love the way I should.
11. The greatest blessing was that God kept us from whole-heartedly pursuing fame and fortune before Byron died.
12. Earline said I acted like an Ahab but did not give in anytime!
13. Do you have divine order in your home? Are you Ahab men and Jezebel women?

HOW ARE CURSES RECOGNIZED THAT COME FROM ANCESTORS?

Even the world can recognize the curses, they just don't know what causes them. For example, suppose the women in a family die of cancer generation after generation. Then we would say that the family is cursed. The next question would be, what is the original sin that started the generational line of cancer? If we can not identify that sin by name, the next best thing to do is to forgive, in general, all ancestors that have sinned and caused this curse.

BLESSINGS AND CURSES

We all live with the results of our actions. Blessings are the result of obeying God. Curses are the result of obeying the Devil - disobeying God.

We already had the blessings in the Garden - now begins the curses of God (Gen. 3:16-19). Pain in childbearing is not something that women suffer alone; her husband suffers emotionally at this time too. The ground is cursed because man gave heed to his wife and obeyed her against God's commandments. Women suffer as they watch the hard, back-breaking or stressful work of their husbands. And so began the power struggle that all men and women engage in.

EARLINE'S TESTIMONY ABOUT HER ANCESTRAL BACKGROUND

I have an Indian - English - German - French background. There are curses on each of these people: Indians worshipped demons; some English and Europeans were Druids - they worshipped Satan.

In innocence or ignorance, my father participated in some occult practices: **wart removal** and **water witching**. He just thought that these were mountain medicine and practices from Tennessee. From my father came curses of Masons and Indians. Physical problems came as a result of curses on Indian worship: inactive thyroid, female disorders and heart disease.

My father removed the warts from my brother by witchcraft. Satan swapped the demon of warts for a demon of spinal meningitis which almost killed him. Satan doesn't give anything away for free; there is a price to pay. He actually went to Heaven and saw two siblings which had died early in life, and then God sent him back to earth.

My mother was a paranoid schizophrenic with an Indian - English background. Her emotional illness caused me to need a lot of deliverance from emotional problems.

HOW ARE CURSES BROKEN?

Once the curse is identified, then you know that there is sin in the camp. The sin must be dealt with by the individual, not the leader. The individual must confess his sins and the sins of the fathers (Lev. 26:40-42). He should then forgive his ancestors, especially his parents, for bringing curses and torment into his life and family. After you have asked God to forgive all parties involved in the sin that brought the curse and repented yourself, then you have a right to break the curse in the Name of Jesus Christ.

WHAT IS DONE AFTER THE CURSE IS BROKEN?

Once the curse is broken, cast out the demons that came in through the curse by their names. After the demons are cast out, pray for physical healing of the body and mental and emotional healing for the mind. After you have been delivered and healed, **Go and Sin no More lest a worse thing come upon you.** You must change your way of thinking and acting even though this curse was brought upon you by your ancestors.

RESULTS OF BREAKING CURSES

We have seen people begin to receive deliverance as the curses were broken but before any demons were verbally cast out in the Name of Jesus Christ. Deliverance sessions become more smooth with less manifestations of demons and violence to the people. When the demons tell us that they have a right to remain because of a curse, we break the curse and then we are able to cast out the demons who refuse to leave.

STEPS TO FREEDOM FROM CURSES

1. **Identify the name** of the curse and the sin that caused the curse.
2. **Repent and pray** to God to take away the right for the curse to be in your life.
3. **Forgive the ancestors** (in ancestral curses) for their sin against you in placing this curse on the family line.
4. **Break the curse** in the Name of Jesus Christ.
5. **Cast out the demons** that came in with the curse.
6. **Discipline your life** and sin no more.

CURSED OBJECTS ON YOU AND IN YOUR HOME

Earline will tell you what she has learned about jewelry. I want the men to take off all religious objects. I want the women to take off all jewelry except for wedding rings and watches. My favorite example is pierced ears which is a sign of slavery in the Bible. Jesus Christ wants us to live a simple life without religious objects or graven images. Cast out of people and houses - command all demons to go by these names or associated with these objects:

Books and objects identified with anything related to Satan's Kingdom.
1. Sinful activities of former residents left **curses**.
2. Knocking or noisy ghosts (poltergeist) and apparitions.
3. Owl and frog images of all types.

4. Witch's mask and fetishes used by witch doctors.
5. Objects and literature that pertain to false religions, cults, the occult and spiritism.
6. Graven images of Gods (demons).
7. Objects dedicated to demons (idols and artifacts).
8. Ouija boards or other occult paraphernalia.
9. Prayers and worship to demons bring **curses** on home.
10. Mexican sun Gods; idols, incense; Buddhas; hand carved objects from Africa or the Orient; anything connected with astrology, horoscopes, fortune telling, etc.; books or objects associated with witchcraft, good luck charms or cult religions (metaphysics, Christian Science, Jehovah's Witnesses, etc.); rock and roll records and tapes.
11. Jewelry given to a person by someone in witchcraft, hex signs, ancient geometric and mystical motifs, jewelry designed to bring good luck and act as talisman to chase evil.
12. Egyptian ankh, broken cross (peace symbol), chais, Polynesian tikkis of Gods, African jujus, Italian horn, protectors from the evil eye, hand with index and little fingers pointing up, crosses, clovers, stars, wishbones, luck coins, mystic medals, horseshoes, religious fetishes and statues.
13. Products with cryptic curses **(hidden secret, occult curses)**.
14. Dolls used for witchcraft and magic; puppets, cult objects or representations.

FIVE STEPS TO CLEANING HOUSE OF CURSED OBJECTS

1. Six-way prayer of forgiveness - you forgive your ancestors, descendants and others, ask God to forgive and bless them. Ask God to forgive you; you forgive yourself for sins against your body. Also ask forgiveness for spiritual adultery.
2. Break curses and soul ties from others (ancestors) and to others (descendants); break curses of psychic or Catholic prayers.
3. Clean out house of those objects or exorcise objects (you do this).
4. Anoint house with oil and cast evil spirits out of house (you do this).
5. Cast demons out of people that came in thru curses from others (optional); for mass deliverance, see Cursed Objects and Demon Infestation.

SUMMARY

1. God cursed the earth when Adam and Eve fell.
2. **Biblical Curses** apply to those or their descendents who have committed these sins.
3. **Curses on Children** can be used when specifically working with children.
4. **Hex Signs** and all associated with these symbols are demonic.

BLESSINGS, CURSES AND DURATION

Exodus 20:1-5 Curse of idol worship extends to **fourth generation** of great grandchildren.
Deut. 23:2 Curse of the bastard extends to **tenth generation** of descendants.
Deut. Ch. 28 Blessings are for obeying and curses for disobeying the Holy Bible; **verses 1-14: blessings, 15-44: curses and 45-68: wrath of God.**

Exodus 20:1-5 & Ezekiel 18:1-9 God showed Earline that this was the curse of idol worship brought on her by her **Indian ancestors** which caused her and her family **heart trouble**. He also showed her how to break the curse.

Notice how a family can be cursed to the fourth or tenth generation by the ancestors. **Actually there are curses on the human race that go all the way back to Adam and Eve.** Blessings can go from generation to generation if not broken by sin. Curses can also go from generation to generation if not broken by prayer.

Very simply, we are **blessed for obeying** the Word of God and **cursed for disobeying** the Word of God. Blessings and curses are promises from God which will either bring down the wrath of God or His favor on your family.

God will supply all of your needs: **mental, physical, spiritual and material**. He can become your **Savior, Baptizer, Healer, Deliverer and Prosperer**. These things will only come to pass if you follow the Bible - **for every promise there is a condition**. If you do not meet the condition, you will not receive the promise!

There is probably a curse for every scripture that is disobeyed. Sixty-six curses are listed under Biblical Curses which follow:

BIBLICAL CURSES (EXCERPTS)
1. Those who curse/mistreat Jews (Deut. 27:26; Gen. 27:29; 12:3; Num. 24:9).
2. Those willing deceivers (Jos. 9:23, Jer. 48:10; Mal. 1:14; Gen. 27:12).
3. An adulterous woman (Numbers 5:27).
4. Disobedience of Lord's commandments (Deut. 11:28; Dan. 9:11; Jer. 11:3).
5. Idolatry (Jer. 44:8; Deut. 29:19; Ex. 20:5; Deut. 5:8-9).
6. Those who keep or own cursed objects (Deut. 7:25; Jos. 6:18).
7. Those who refuse to come to the Lord's help (Judges 5:23).
8. House of the wicked (Prov. 3:33).
9. He who gives not to the poor (Prov. 28:27).
10. The earth by reason of man's disobedience (Isa. 24:3-6).
11. Jerusalem is a curse to all nations if Jews rebel against God (Jer. 26:6).
12. Thieves and those who swear falsely by the Lord's Name (Zech. 5:4).
13. Ministers who fail to give the glory to God (Mal. 2:2; Rev. 1:6).
14. Those who rob God of tithes and offerings (Mal. 3:9; Haggai 1:6-9).
15. Those who hearken unto their wives rather than God (Gen. 3:17).
16. Those who lightly esteem their parents (Deut. 27:16).
17. Those who make graven images (Deut. 5:8; 27:15, Ex. 20:4).
18. Those who willfully cheat people out of their property (Deut. 27:17).
19. Those who take advantage of the blind (Deut. 27:18).
20. Those oppressing strangers, widows, fatherless (Deut. 27:19; Ex. 22:22-24)
21. Him who lies with his father's wife (Deut. 27:20; Lev. 18:8).
22. Him who lies with his sister (Deut. 27:22).
23. Those who smite their neighbors secretly (Deut. 27:24).
24. Those who take money to slay the innocent (Deut. 27:24).

25. Him who lies with any beast (Deut. 27:21; Ex. 22:19).
26. Adulterers (Job 24:15-18).
27. The proud (Psalm 119:21).
28. Those who trust in man and not the Lord (Jer. 48:10).
29. Those who do the work of the Lord deceitfully (Jer. 48:10).
30. Him who keeps back his sword from blood (Jer. 48:10; I Kings 20:35-42).
31. Those who reward evil for good (Prov. 17:13).
32. Illegitimate children (Deut. 23:2).
33. Children born from incestuous unions (Gen. 19:36-38).
34. Murderers (Exodus 21:12).
35. To murder indirectly (Exodus 21:14).
36. Children who strike their parents (Exodus 21:15).
37. Kidnappers (Exodus 21:16; Deut. 24:7).
38. Those who curse their parents (Exodus 21:17).
39. Those who cause the unborn to die (Exodus 21:22-23).
40. Those who do not prevent death (Exodus 21:29).
41. Those involved in witchcraft (Exodus 22:18).
42. Those who sacrifice to false Gods (Exodus 22:20).
43. Those who attempt to turn anyone away from the Lord (Deut. 13:6-9).
44. Those who follow horoscopes (Deut. 17:2-5).
45. Those who rebel against pastors (Deut. 17:12).
46. False prophets (Deut. 18:19-22).
47. Women who keep not their virginity until they are married (Deut. 22:13-21)
48. Adulterers (Deut. 22:22-27).
49. Parents who do not discipline their children, but honor them above God (I Sam. 2:17, 27-36).
50. Those who curse their rulers (I Kings 2:8-9; Ex. 22:28).
51. Those who teach rebellion against the Lord (Jer. 28:16-17).
52. Those who refuse to warn them that sin (Ezek. 3:18-21).
53. Those who defile the Sabbath (Ex. 31:14; Num. 15:32-36).
54. Those who sacrifice human beings (Lev. 20:2).
55. Participants in séances and fortune telling (Lev. 20:6).
56. Homosexual and lesbian relationships (Lev. 20:13).
57. Sexual intercourse during menstruation (Lev. 20:18).
58. Necromancers and fortune tellers (Lev. 20:27).
59. Those who blaspheme the Lord's name (Lev. 24:15-16).
60. Those who are carnally minded (Romans 8:6).
61. Sodomy (oral and anal sex) (Gen. 19:13, 24-25).
62. Rebellious children (Deut. 21:18-21).
63. Possibly from murder, nonproductivity, a fugitive, vagabond (Gen. 4:11; Matt. 5:21-22, Jesus' statement on hatred equals murder, John 3:15).
64. Possible curse upon improper family structure - destruction of family priesthood (Mal. 4:6) with special attention given to the relationship between father and children.
65. The curse causeless shall not come (Prov. 26:2).
66. Any sin worthy of death is also cursed by God (Deut. 21:22-23).

CURSES ON CHILDREN
1. Children born from incestuous unions (Gen. 19:36-38).
2. Curse of idol worship extends to **fourth generation** of great grandchildren (Exodus 20:1-5).
3. Children who strike their parents (Exodus 21:15).
4. Those who curse their parents (Exodus 21:17).
5. Iniquity of fathers on children (Exodus 34:6-7).
6. Children wandered for forty years (Numbers 14:18 & 33).
7. Idol worship (Deut. 5:9-10).
8. Rebellious children (Deut. 21:18-21).
9. Curse of the bastard extends to **tenth generation** of descendants (Deut. 23:2).
10. In son's days evil will come on his house (I Kings 21:19).
11. The iniquity of the father upon the children (Jer. 32:18).

A CURSE AGAINST PROTESTANTS (EXCERPTS)
One of the authorized curses published in the Romish Pontifical, to be used against Protestants, reads as follows: **May God Almighty and all His saints curse them with the curse with which the devil and his angels are cursed.**

Let all they have be cursed. Always and everywhere let them be cursed. Speaking and silent let them be cursed. Within and without let them be cursed.

From the crown of the head to the sole of the foot let them be cursed. Let all the members of their body be cursed.

Cursed let them be, standing or lying, from this time forth forever; and thus let their candle be extinguished in the presence of God, at the day of judgement.

This is the spirit of Papacy; and all who possess the spirit of the true Christ should readily recognize so base a counterfeit.

CURSES (EXCERPTS)
1. Christians walking in the knowledge and power of their spiritual authority are especially targeted for attention by the enemy.
2. Higher level witches will **scan** the person on whom the curse is to be placed.
3. For example: a woman whose parents were witches was hesitant to break curses and send them back to the source for fear they were coming from her relatives in witchcraft.
4. For some reason women seem more susceptible than men to attack through curses.
5. God's chain of command establishes the father, the husband or the male members of the Christian assembly as a spiritual covering and counseling resource for the women.
6. People often state that they are not under any curses. As regarding final salvation, no; but as far as your life here and now, yes; you definitely can be affected.
7. When man broke God's law and brought black people from Africa to America as slaves, it opened the way for many curses.

8. You cannot get away from judgement for breaking God's laws. Even to this day, Louisiana is ruled by the Prince of Southern Curses and Arkansas by the Prince of the Occult.

9. Those from the northern United States have forbearers in Europe who brought witchcraft curses from the Black Forest, Scandinavia and the Druids in England.

10. When you came into contact with occult practices (such as the Ouija board, horoscopes, fortune tellers, hypnosis, or ESP), you were cursed, your children were cursed, your grandchildren were cursed and your great grandchildren were cursed, all in one operation!

11. Anything in the occult realm requires two steps to destroy the grounds for attack.

12. People ask if every single occult contact will open the door to Satan.

13. Take no chances, just state, **I am closing any door I may have opened to you, Satan, through contact with the Ouija board, astrology, fortune telling, hypnosis, ESP, etc.**.

14. Because you or someone else opened the door to invite attack, you are now legally closing that door and putting Satan on notice about it.

15. The occult is a deadly and dangerous area.

16. Most people are unaware that the witches in Africa have been fasting thirty and forty days to break-up Christian marriages in Africa and this country, especially those among the leadership.

17. One thing to remember about fasting is that basically it opens one to the spirit world.

18. When on a fast, check everything very carefully. There are two stations broadcasting.

19. A curse causeless cannot come, therefore, when they do hit we must seek out the reason and eliminate it.

20. A curse from the law comes from attempting to obey the letter of the law rather than trusting in the Lord.

21. Christ redeems those who put their trust in Him (Deut. 11:28; 26:16; Gal. 3:10-15).

22. If you suspect a curse is rooted in the occult, it must be broken back to at least four generations.

23. When a demon seems to resist the breaking of a curse, break it back fifteen or twenty generations.

24. Never hesitate to break a curse for it is quite simple.

25. We must destroy the curses for they are all around us to entangle and hinder.

26. Some say they want no part of it, but there is a curse on those who will not fight or are slack in the Lord's battle (Jud. 5:23; Jer. 48:10).

27. Seeing to the needs of the poor doesn't mean to be a gullible goose, but to be prayerful and see exactly what God wants you to do.

28. What would have happened to the good Samaritan if he had helped everyone he saw in need on the road that day?

29. We must tune in with the Lord's will and follow Him to discover which persons are our responsibility; those He has equipped you to minister to financially, spiritually and in every way.

30. These will fritter away all your money and God will still judge you for foolish interference.

31. There is a curse on ministers and any believer who will not give glory to Christ (Mal. 2:2; Rev. 1:6).

32. If the wrong kind of people **pray** for you, it can hit you like a curse.
33. There is charismatic witchcraft, also, and often you find groups presided over by a charismatic witch.
34. Stay very close to God's written Word, let everything else be strictly supplementary, to be checked and cross-checked by the Word of God.
35. There is a curse on improper family structure which causes defective family priesthoods (Mal. 4:6).
36. There is a curse from trusting in man instead of God, depending on the flesh instead of the spirit (Jer. 17).
37. Of course some are more susceptible than others, and you need to become aware of where you are weak and brace against it.
38. In sexual areas there are many kinds of curses which can cause trouble.

VOWS AND CURSES (EXCERPTS)

In the Bible, vows were solemn promises to God, either positive or negative. Under the Mosaic Law, the vows and promises of dependents such as children, unmarried daughters and wives were void, except when ratified by the express or tacit consent of the father or husband. This afforded protection to them against rash vows. The whole matter is explored in Numbers 30. Other scriptures dealing with vows include: Ecc. 5'4-6; Num. 30:2; Deut. 23:21-22).

Broken vows can be a source of real trouble. That is why Jonah repented and renewed his vows in the belly of the fish, saying, **I will pay my vows**. If a vow is discovered to be contrary to scripture and dishonoring to God, it should be formally renounced and forgiveness sought for making it (I John 1:9). A vow that is expressly evil or is for an evil purpose should never be made nor kept. To keep such a vow, for the sake of consistency, is to compound one evil by another (Matt. 5:33-37).

A curse has been defined as: uttering a wish of evil against one; to imprecate evil; to call for mischief or injury to fall upon; to execrate, to bring evil upon or to; to blast, vex harass or torment with great calamities.

We have found that even the wrong kinds of **prayer** and laying on of hands, or **prayers** at a distance, have resulted in hurtful and dismaying results with the effects of a curse. For example: Curses came on a man and woman through a couple who were casting witchcraft curses in a Full Gospel Church!

HEX SIGNS (EXCERPTS)

The five pointed star has been used by witches for centuries and called the pentacle or pentagram. With the two points up (as in Eastern Star) it is called the sign of the goat or Satan; one point up symbolizes witchcraft. When witches want to talk with demons, they will often stand within a pentagram and the demon will appear within a six pointed star by two triangles (hexagram) commonly called the Star of David. The Mogen David, as it was called, was a Cabalistic magic symbol for white magic and the word hex comes from the hexagram.

All Masonic symbols were ancient witchcraft signs long before freemasonry was created. The initiation rituals for witchcraft and for Masons are identical (according to ex-witch John Todd), again demonstrating Masonic roots into witchcraft. The only difference is that the initiated witch disrobes completely at the close, and signs in his own blood.

The wiggly horn called the Italian horn is also a witchcraft device (leprechaun's staff or unicorn's horn) and means you trust the Devil for your finances.

The Egyptian ankh (cross with a loop on top) is a sex Goddess symbol meaning you despise virginity, believe in fertility rites, and worship and serve the Egyptian sun God RA (Egyptian name for Lucifer).

All the signs of the Zodiac are occult symbols as are the little Mexican sun Gods and Buddhas. The crescent moon and star are the sign of an initiate into witchcraft.

In the Old Testament, God gave cunning skills to hands of artisans who fashioned the furnishings and decorations for the tabernacle. The use of these signs and symbols, and others which are the property of Satan can bring demons to your home and/or person.

Neither shalt thou bring an abomination into thine house lest thou be a cursed thing like it; but thou shalt utterly abhor it for it is a cursed thing (Deut. 7:26).

SYMBOLS OF HEX SIGNS (EXCERPTS)

Remove these symbols from your person and possessions:
1. Six Petal Rosette and Lucky Stars - these are your lucky stars.
2. The Irish Shamrock Hex - good luck, fast life, good fortune and fidelity.
3. Tulip - faith, hope and charity.
4. Unicorn - virtue and piety.
5. Fertility.
6. Twelve Petal Rosette - that each month of the year be joyous ones.
7. The Distelfink - the bird of happiness always near you and good fortune.
8. Your Lucky Stars - lucky stars that guide your heart.
9. Love and Romance - rosette and hearts of love and romance.
10. Eight Pointed Star - star and rosette to bring abundance and goodwill.
11. Friendship.
12. There is a symbol for each of the above listed hex signs.

BREAKING CURSES
I break any curses placed on me or my descendants from uttering a wish of evil against one; to imprecate evil, to call for mischief or injury to fall upon; to execrate, to bring evil upon or to; to blast, vex, harass or torment with great calamities. I break these curses in Jesus' name. I break the curses back to ten generations or even to Adam and Eve on both sides of my family, and destroy every legal hold and every legal ground that demons have to work in my life. I break curses that follow in the name of the Lord Jesus Christ.

Mistreating God's Chosen People	Willing Deceivers
Adultery, Harlotry, Prostitution	Disobedience to Bible
Idolatry	Keeping Cursed Objects
Refusing To Fight For God	House of Wicked
Not Giving To Poor	Stealing
Swearing Falsely By God	Failing To Give Glory to God
Robbing God of Tithes	Dishonoring Parents
Hearkening to Wives Rather Than God	Making Graven Images
Cheating People Out of Property	Taking Advantage of Blind
Oppressing Strangers, Widows, Orphans	Bestiality
Incest With Sister or Mother	Murder Secretly or For Hire
Pride	Putting Trust In Man
Doing The Work of God Deceitfully	Rewarding Evil For Good
Abortion or Causing Unborn To Die	Having Bastards
Murdering Indirectly	Striking Parents
Kidnapping	Cursing Parents
Not Preventing Death	Sacrificing to Gods
Witchcraft	Turning Someone Away From God
Following Horoscopes	Rebelling Against Pastors
Losing Virginity Before Marriage	False Prophets
Rape	Not Disciplining Children
Teaching Rebellion Against God	Cursing Rulers
Refusing To Warn Sinners	Defiling The Sabbath
Sacrificing Humans	Seances and Fortune Telling
Intercourse During Menstruation	Homosexuals and Lesbians
Necromancers	Blaspheming Lord's Name
Being Carnally Minded	Oral and Anal Sex
Children Rebelling	Nonproductivity
Fugitive and Vagabond	Improper Family Structure
Destruction of Family Priesthood	Refusing To Do The Word of God
Family Disorder	Failure and Poverty
Any Sin Worthy of Death	Touching God's Anointed
Offending Children Believing Christ	Loving Cursing
Choosing That Which God Delights Not In	Looking To World For Help
Adding To or Taking Away From Bible	Stubbornness and Rebellion
Any Biblical Curse Not listed Above	Perversion of Gospel

Failure to hearken unto the voice of the Lord God, to observe to do all His commandments and His statutes; then all these curses shall come upon thee, and overtake thee.

DEMONS SENT BY BIBLICAL CURSES

Pestilence	Idol Worship	Graven Images
Consumption	Bastard	Pride
Fever	Wicked Balances	Catholic Prayers
Inflammation	Dislike/Hatred/Murder	Prince Southern Curses

Extreme Burning	Curse of the Law	Prince of Occult
Blasting	Bless You Spirits	Witchcraft Curses
Mildew	Incest	Voodoo Curses
Botch of Egypt	Lesbians	Occult Curses
Emerods	Necromancers	American Indian Curses
Scab	Blaspheming	Charismatic Witchcraft
Itch	Sodomy	Horoscopes
Madness	Oral & Anal Sex	Rebellion
Blindness	Slackness	False Prophets
Astonishment of Heart	Deeper Teachings	Seances
Plagues	Irish Shamrock Hex	Fortune Telling
Sore Sicknesses	Fertility	Nonproductivity
Diseases of Egypt	Deceiving	Personal Poverty
Trembling of Heart	Adultery	Misrepresentation
Failing of Eyes	Disobedience	Perversion of Judgment
Sorrow of Mind	Cursed Objects	Doubt
Broken Vows	Thievery	Homosexual
Unicorn	False Swearing	Tulip
Twelve Petal Rosette	The Distelfink	Your Lucky Stars
Love & Romance	Eight Pointed Star	Friendship Hex
Pentacle/Pentagram	Eastern Star	Hexagram
Star of David	Mogen David	Cabalistic Magic Symbol
White Magic	Masonic Symbols	Freemasonry
Italian Horn	Leprechaun's Staff	Unicorn's Horn
Egyptian Ankh	Egyptian Sun God RA	Zodiac
Mexican Sun God	Buddhas	Crescent Moon & Star

Cursing, Vexation, Rebuke, Destroying, Perishing, Consuming, Groping
Not Prosper, Oppressed, Spoiled, Failure, Crushed, Smite, Pursuing
Sore Botch of Knees, Legs and Whole Body
Overtaking, Distress, Plucked, Chastisement, Removed, Not Healed
Astonishment, Proverb, Byword, Want, Besiege, Straitness, Evil

REFERENCES

Eleven books written by Win Worley, Hegewisch Baptist Church, Highland, Indiana.

SECTION 3 PRAYERS AND LISTS OF CURSE DEMONS

CONTENTS
1. OVERALL PRAYER
2. OVERALL COMMANDS
3. WORD CURSES
    1. Christian Fantasy Prayer
    2. Lies, Deceit And Flattery Prayer
    3. List Of Demons
        1. Christian Fantasy - Lies Not Truth
        2. Lies, Deceit And Flattery
        3. Bad Habits Of Thinking And Reacting
4. BIBLICAL CURSES
    1. Prayer
    2. List of demons
5. AMERICAN INDIAN CURSES
    1. Prayer
    2. List Of Demons
6. ALASKAN NATIVE CURSES
    1. Prayer To Break Curses
    2. Prayer
    3. List Of Demons
7. AFRICAN AMERICAN CURSES
    1. Breaking The Willie Lynch Curse Prayer
        1. Deliverance
    2. Walls Of Argument Prayer
        1. Deliverance
    3. List Of Demons
        1. Sins / Curses / Demons
    2. Various Demons
    3. Sex
    4. Infirmity
    5. Death
    6. Religion
    7. Addictions
    8. Slavery
    9. Black Interaction
    10. Occult
    11. Black
    12. Demonic Tongues
    13. Matriarchal
8. CURSING OTHERS AND BEING CURSED
    1. Prayer
    2. List Of Demons
9. ARE YOU LIVING WITH A CURSE?

            1. Commands
    10. **CURSES FOR SHEDDING INNOCENT BLOOD**
        1. Prayer
        2. List Of Demons
    11. **HOUSE CURSES**
        1. Cleaning Your House Prayer
    12. **CURSE OF PRIDE**
        1. Prayer
        2. List Of Demons
    13. **CURSE OF AHAB AND JEZEBEL**
        1. Prayer
        2. Ahab And Jezebel Demons Short List
            1. Ahab Demons
            2. Jezebel Demons
        3. Ahab And Jezebel Demons Long List
            1. Ahab Demons
            2. Jezebel Demons

OVERALL PRAYER

Almighty God, please forgive us for omission - commission, known - unknown, deliberate - inadvertent sins by the blood of Jesus Christ. We thank God for power and authority over the enemy: satan and his kingdom. We are strong in the Lord and the power of his might. We cover us with the blood of Jesus Christ. We pray the Holy Bible and ask in the name of Jesus Christ, Lord, master & savior. Amen! So be it!

OVERALL COMMANDS

We use the power of God given to believers. We take authority over the kingdom of evil. We bind and subdue satan's empire. We enter into spiritual warfare and assault the kingdom of darkness. We bind the forces of evil and destroy the kingdom of evil. We send legions of warring angels to attack. We use every verse in the Holy Bible that wars against the demonic forces. We bind principalities, powers, rulers of darkness of this world and spiritual wickedness in high places.

WORD CURSES
Christian Fantasy Prayer

I forgive those who have controlled me with charismatic witchcraft. Please forgive me for practicing witchcraft and trying to control other people's wills. I take authority over these evil forces, break evil soul ties and break curses placed on me. I command these spirits to come out of me.

Lies, Deceit And Flattery Prayer

Father, I want to be like you; you do not lie. I want The Truth to be in me. I repent for being a liar, a deceitful person, being a cheat and dishonest, flattering other people, giving a false appearance, having pride, ego and vanity, being false and faithless, pretending I am something other than what I am, and for falseness of dress, thoughts and actions. Help me to be what you made me to be; I want to be natural and not false.

LIST OF DEMONS
Christian Fantasy - Lies Not Truth

Christian Fantasy and Fables, Christian Tradition and Cliches, Lies, Lying, Deceit, Deception, Ignorance, Laziness, Slothfulness, Playing Church, Play Acting, Lying Teachers and Prophets, False Witness, Falsehood, Pat Phrases, Soulish Prophecy, Spiritual Adultery, False Dreams and Visions, Charismatic Witches and Warlocks, False Prophetesses, Hypocrisy, Vile Affections, Theatrics, Sophistication, Pretension, Divination, False Gifts and Fruits, Greed, Gluttony, Drunkenness, Mind Control, Witchcraft and Rebellion.

Lies, Deceit And Flattery

Lies, Lying, Prevarication, Equivocation, Paltering, Fibbing, Deceitfulness, Deceptiveness, Trickery, Misleading, Deluding, Beguiling, Dishonesty, Unfairness, Mendacious, Untruthful, Flattery, Feigning, Pride, Ego, Vanity, Falseness, Imprudent, Unwise, Faithless, Cheating, Pretending, Insecurity, Inferiority, Rejection, Bitterness, Rebellion, Selfishness, Greediness, Self-Serving, False Witnesses, False Teachers, False Prophets, Fruit of Their Lies, Self-Centered, Spiritual Adultery, Love of Money, Lust of the Eyes, Lust of the Flesh, Pride of Life, Compulsive Liar, Christian Fantasy, Affectation, Theatrics, Playacting, Sophistication, Pretension and Self-Inflated.

Bad Habits Of Thinking And Reacting

Fear of Rejection, Dread, Shame, Fear of Men's Opinions, Apprehension, Sexual Impurity, Fear of Disapproval, Roving, Cult Involvement, Bitterness, Restlessness, Embarrassment, Rebellion, Unreality, Self-Will, Stubbornness, Indifference, Disgust, Anti-Submissiveness, Passivity of Mind, Worry, Disobedience, Lethargy, Anxiety, Fear of Criticism, Depression, Fear of Reproof, Insecurity, Discouragement, Fear of Confrontation, Timidity, Defeatism, Confusion, Inadequacy, Hopelessness, Doubt, Ineptness, Heaviness, Unbelief, Distrust, Burden, Indecision, Fantasy, Forgetfulness, Procrastination, Compromise, Rationalization, Pride, Fear of Failure, Deception, Play-Acting, Ego, Discontent, Frustration, Pretense, Fatigue, Hyperactivity, Argument, Selfishness, Carelessness, Mockery, Hypocrisy, Heedlessness, Cynicism, Smug Complacency.

BIBLICAL CURSES
Prayer

I forgive my ancestors and anyone else that has cursed me. I break curses placed on me or my descendants from uttering a wish of evil against one; to imprecate evil, to call for mischief or injury to fall upon; to execrate, to bring evil upon or to; to blast, vex, harass or torment with great calamities. I break these curses. I break the curses back to ten generations or even to Adam and Eve on both sides of my family, and destroy legal holds and legal grounds that demons have to work in my life.

I now rebuke, break, loose myself and my children from evil curses, charms, vexes, hexes, spells, jinxes, psychic powers, bewitchment, witchcraft and sorcery, that have been put upon me or my family line from persons or from occult or psychic sources, and I cancel connected or related spirits and command them to leave me. I thank you for setting me free.

List Of Demons

- Mistreating GOD's Chosen People
- Adultery, Harlotry, Prostitution
- Idolatry
- Refusing To Fight For GOD
- Not Giving To Poor
- Swearing Falsely By GOD
- Robbing GOD of Tithes
- Hearkening to Wives Rather Than GOD
- Cheating People Out of Property
- Oppressing Strangers, Widows, Orphans
- Incest With Sister or Mother
- Pride
- Doing The Work of GOD Deceitfully
- Abortion or Causing Unborn To Die
- Murdering Indirectly
- Kidnapping
- Not Preventing Death
- Witchcraft
- Following Horoscopes
- Losing Virginity Before Marriage
- Rape
- Teaching Rebellion Against GOD
- Refusing To Warn Sinners
- Sacrificing Humans
- Intercourse During Menstruation
- Necromancers
- Being Carnally Minded
- Children Rebelling
- Fugitive and Vagabond
- Destruction of Family Priesthood
- Family Disorder
- **Sin Worthy of Death**
- **Biblical Curses Not listed Above**
- **Choosing That Which GOD Delights Not**
- **In Offending Children Believing CHRIST**
- **Adding To or Taking Away From Bible**
- Willing Deceivers
- Disobedience to Bible
- Keeping Cursed Objects
- House of Wicked
- Stealing
- Failing To Give Glory to GOD
- Dishonoring Parents
- Making Graven Images
- Taking Advantage of Blind
- Bestiality
- Murder Secretly or For Hire
- Putting Trust In Man
- Rewarding Evil For Good
- Having Bastards
- Striking Parents
- Cursing Parents
- Sacrificing to Gods
- Turning Someone Away From GOD
- Rebelling Against Pastors
- False Prophets
- Not Disciplining Children
- Cursing Rulers
- Defiling The Sabbath
- Seances and Fortune Telling
- Homosexuals and Lesbians
- Blaspheming LORD'S NAME
- Oral and Anal Sex
- Nonproductivity
- Improper Family Structure
- Refusing To Do THE WORD OF GOD
- Failure and Poverty
- Touching GOD's Anointed
- Perversion of Gospel
- Looking To World For Help
- Stubbornness and Rebellion
- Loving Cursing

Pestilence, Idol Worship, Graven Images, Consumption, Bastard, Pride, Fever, Wicked Balances, Catholic Prayers, Inflammation, Dislike / Hatred / Murder, Prince of Southern Curses, Extreme Burning, Curse of the Law, Prince of Occult, Blasting, Bless You Spirits, Witchcraft Curses, Mildew, Incest, Voodoo Curses, Botch of Egypt, Lesbians, Occult Curses, Emerods, Necromancers, American Indian Curses, Scab, Blaspheming,

Charismatic Witchcraft, Itch, Sodomy, Horoscopes, Madness, Oral and Anal Sex, Rebellion, Blindness, Slackness, False Prophets, Astonishment of Heart, Deeper Teachings, Seances, Plagues, Irish Shamrock Hex, Fortune Telling, Sore Sicknesses, Fertility, Nonproductivity, Diseases of Egypt, Deceiving, Personal Poverty, Trembling of Heart, Adultery, Misrepresentation, Failing Eyes, Disobedience, Perversion of Judgment, Sorrow of Mind, Cursed Objects, Doubt, Broken Vows, Thievery, Homosexual, Unicorn, False Swearing, Tulip, Twelve Petal Rosette, The Distelfink, Your Lucky Stars, Love and Romance, Eight Pointed Star, Friendship Hex, Pentacle / Pentagram, Eastern Star, Hexagram, Star of David, Mogen David, Cabalistic Magic Symbol, White Magic, Masonic Symbols, Freemasonry, Italian Horn, Leprechaun's Staff, Unicorn's Horn, Egyptian Ankh, Egyptian Sun God RA, Zodiac, Mexican Sun God, Buddhas, Crescent Moon and Star; Cursing, Vexation, Rebuke, Destroying, Perishing, Consuming, Groping; Not Prospering, Oppressed, Spoiled, Failure, Crushed, Smite, Pursuing; Sore Botch of Knees, Legs and Whole Body; Overtaking, Distress, Plucked, Chastisement, Removed, Not Healed; Astonishment, Proverb, Byword, Want, Besiege, Straitness, Evil.

AMERICAN INDIAN CURSES
Prayer

I forgive American Indians and my Indian ancestors for witchcraft against the white man, me and my relatives; for deep-hidden-seething anger-bitterness-resentment-hatred of the white man; for cursing the land and people; for eating and drinking flesh and blood; and for worshipping demons. I forgive the white man for rejecting and enslaving them on the reservation. I forgive the war women for the Jezebelic matriarchal rule of the tribe.

I forgive the witch doctors and shamans for cursing the descendents, dedicating them to Satan, and causing physical problems and diseases. I forgive my ancestors.

I ask forgiveness for myself for the sin of idol worship and disobedience as described in Exodus 20, Leviticus 26 and Ezekiel 18. I ask you to forgive me for sins associated with Indians such as Scouting. I will destroy Indian artifacts, break ungodly soul ties and break ties to Indian organizations.

I break the curses of incest, rape, immorality and the bastard. I break spiritual roots to diseases brought about by curses. I break American Indian curses on me and my descendents back to when the white man came to America.

I come against spirits that have been renounced and legal rights taken away; I command that they come out with their families and works as their names are called.

List Of Demons

Alcoholic spirits (especially firewater & whiskey)
Akeyla (Sun God)
Astrology
Anger
Ancestor Gods

Break curse of loss of prosperity
Blood brothers & sisters (break ties)
Baby Pow
Baby Pow Reincarnation
Baal Worship
Beads (white - peace; purple - war,

Aiy
Anti-Christ
Amulets
BatGod - Jaguar
Buffalo
Buffalo child (Croaton)
Blood thirsty
Curse of firstborn to pass
 thru the fire
Child sacrifice
Charms (war, health, ward
 off evil spirits)
Chac (water God)
Drums
Dominance
Dances (owl, charcoal, sun, demon.)
 snake, duck, chicken,
 horse, fire leaping, fish,
 alligator, crow, ghost,
 buffalo, scalp)
Desertion
Elk Spirits
Divorce
Eliminate curse American Indians
Earth Mother
Eagle
Estsanatlehi (old woman
 who rejuvenates self)
Earth monster Tlalal-tecuhtli
Hiawatha (glandular mal-
 functions, swelling)
Father sky
Fox spirit (makes a witch
 pass thru fire)
Fireside dancer
Fear of lack of provision
False prophecy thru money
False Indian prophecy
False tongues
Feathers
Firebird
FireGod (Xiutechli)
Great Buffalo spirit
God of War (Ojibway)
God of The Air (Ojibway)
God of The Stars (Ojibway)

death or mourning)
BirdGod (Crocodile)
Bitterness
Cannibalism (Ojibway, Medicine Man)
Caribou spirit
Curse on Arrowhead
Curse to cause cutting off
Hopa doll
Indian rituals
Hypnotic trance
Idol worship
Incantation
Indian Astrology spirits (believed to
be ruling spirits) when a star comes
earth, it is believed to change into

Indian Art
Indian artifacts
Indian chants
Indian corn
Indian curses
Indian drumbeat (Voodoo worship)
Indian eye
Indian Fireside Humor spirit (Sioux)
Indian folklore
Indian Jezebel
Indian Magic (arrowheads, string, gourd
rattles, rawhide, roots, twigs, berries
beaks of birds, bird wings, pure white
pebbles, turquoise, eagles, blackbirds,
peace pipe, bones)
Indian magic spirits
Indian Mythology spirits (for youth)
Indian pierced ear spirit
Indian pierced ears in women, men and
children
Indian scalp spirit
Indian spirit of bondage
Indian spirit of poverty
Indian spirit of war
Indian Sorcery
Indian witchcraft (ability to turn ones-
self into a bear, wolf, fox, owl, snake)
Inherited incest
Knives
Ka-du-te-ta (older women who never die)

God of Herbs of The Earth
  (Ojibway)
Great Spirit
Great Lodge
Great White Father
God of The Harvest
God of Death (Aztec) asso-
  ciated with group KISS
Geronimo
God's eye
Great Father
God of Hunting (Ojibway)
Greed
Heavy heart
Human sacrifice
Hoop dance
Horoscopes
Hatred
Peyote eating (open to drug
  spirits)
Power over life of animals
Power over death of animals
  (esp. wolf) Crow medicine men
Peace piper
Peace pipe worship (Calumet)
Poverty
Pow-wow
Prayer to the Dead (Winnebago,
  Peyote cult)
Pride
Priesthood of the Bow
Rejection
Raccoon spirits
Reincarnation
Raindance
Rebellion
Resentment
Retaliation
Religious spirits (prophets, priests)
Regeneration, green corn dance
Sacrifice to God of The Harvest
Sacrificial pole
Scout Idols
Scout Oaths
Scout Societies
Seances(Croaton)

Kachina doll
Lenelanapa (Indian Macho man)
Longhouse
Maid of the Mist
Masks for dances
Matolu (chief)
Medicine Bag
Medicine Lodge
Medicine Man
Medicine tipis
Mediums
Moloch
Moon worship
Mother earth
Murder
Nakedness
Necromancy (Ojibway & Cherokee)
Order of the Arrow
Spirit of the Sky
Spirit of the Moon
Spirit of Happy Hunting
  (powerful death spirit)
Spirit of Animals
Spirit of Trees
Spirit of Grass
Spirit of Water
Spirit of Stones
Spirit of Maize
Spirit of Maple Syrup in trees
Spirit of Nature Worship
Spirit Guides
Squash Blossom
Squirrel Spirits
Stag
Stooped shoulder
Superstition
Submission to tribal custom
Sweat lodges & puberty rites
Teepee
Thief
Thunderbird (Eagle) no head, beak full
  of rows of wolf's teeth, **powerful
  ruling spirit in American Indians**)
Sisuitl (soul catcher)
Thunder God (Ibeorhum)
Tobacco Spirits (nicotine, cigarettes,

Serpent swastika
Shamans (medicine man) seer
Sitting Bull
Si-ka-ma-hi-fi (Elder creator spirit, Hidatsa)
Snake dance
Song to the Morning Star (Pawnee)
Sorcery
Sun worship
Sun Dance (all)
Spirit of the Prairie wolf
Spirit of the Sun
Spirit of the Clouds
cigar)
Totem pole (Spirit of Theclan)
War God
Warpath
War Whoops
Wigwam (Ojibway)
Will of Wisp
Woe from long march (Mohawk), Six Nations
Wolf
Break curses of Half Breed

ALASKAN NATIVE CURSES
Prayer To Break Curses

I forgive my ancestors and descendents; I ask You to forgive me and I forgive myself for sins which bring these curses on me. I break the following curses:
exotic and old diseases, and new viruses, AIDS, ebola and ecoli
killer bees, ants, locusts and flies bringing devastation and disease
sin, trespass, disobedience and iniquity
cover up, act secretly and treacherously
moral, social, spiritual and land hardships
reverse prejudice, racism, division, rebellion and loneliness
prehistoric terrorism
pain, terror and defilement
attacks of earthly leaders and demonic powers
anger, frustration, resentment, bitterness, revenge and pride
disease, domestic violence, hatred and broken relationships
child, spouse, drug and alcohol, and financial and substance abuse
hallucinogenic drug in peyote

Prayer

I forgive my ancestors, descendents and others, ask you to forgive me and I forgive myself for worshiping traditions and idols, alcohol and drug abuse, rape, sexual abuse and perversion, murder, self bitterness and hatred, occult, Americans and religions for suppressing religious and cultural practices, having to depend on welfare, reversing gender roles; multiple spouses; **false religions and demonic beliefs, ceremonies, dances and rituals, having demonic paraphernalia, talismans, amulets, charms, spirit poles, objects, adornment and tattoos;** sins of Alaskan Natives, Indians and Eskimos; **Russians, traders, soldiers and others for mistreating my ancestors;** those who brought alcoholism, drug addiction, heart disease, diabetes, fetal alcohol syndrome, serious abuse of women and children, incarceration and suicide upon my people; **being warlike, taking slaves, barbarism, torture and cruelty;** following shamans and wise men; for worshiping and following demons; **tribes, clans and groups for their demonic beliefs;** preferential female infanticide; following myths and legends; **transvestites,**

adultery, wife swapping and incest; seeking help from evil spirits; **worshipping animals and their spirits;** reincarnation and ancestor worship; acquiring guardian spirits; seeking forbidden knowledge; demonic healing and divination; worship of nature and earth; **transformation into animals and animals into humans;** fears of death and shamans; mistreating and killing slaves; cutting the flesh; using human fat and mummies; magic and witchcraft; superstition and taboos; **insanity, severe sickness, early death and diseases of Alaska. We come against spirits that have been renounced and legal rights taken away, and command that they come out with their families and works as their names are called.**

List Of Demons

Rape, sexual abuse, sexual perversion, murder, self bitterness, self hatred, occultism, welfare dependence, reversing gender roles, multiple marriages, **false religions, demonic traditions, beliefs, ceremonies, dances and rituals;** slavery, **having demonic paraphernalia, talismans, amulets, charms, spirit poles, objects, adornment and tattoos;** Alaskan Native, Indian and Eskimo spirits; **alcoholism, drug addiction, heart disease, diabetes, fetal alcohol syndrome, abuse of women and children, incarceration and suicide;** barbarism, torture and cruelty; following shamans and wise men; worshiping demons; **tribe, clan and group spirits;** female infanticide; following myths and legends; **transvestites, adultery, wife swapping and incest;** seeking help from evil spirits; reincarnation and ancestor worship; animism, guardian spirits; seeking forbidden knowledge; demonic healing and divination; worship of nature; **transformation into animals and animals into humans;** fears of death and shamans; cutting of the flesh; using human fat and mummies; magic and witchcraft; superstition and taboos; **insanity, sickness, death and diseases of Alaska.**

AFRICAN AMERICAN CURSES
Breaking The Willie Lynch Curse Prayer

I forgive Willie Lynch and those involved in slave trade and slave use throughout time whether in the Black or White Race. I forgive those who treat the Black Race as slaves today. I forgive those who want to lynch me personally, ministerially and business-wise today. I pray that you would forgive and bless them with spiritual blessings, especially salvation.

I break the curse of Willie Lynch off of me and my bloodline going back to 1712 and earlier. I now break curses placed on me by those involved in slavery and those who treat me like a slave. I command the demons restore to me and my family what they have stolen from us.

Deliverance

I now command demons whose legal right has been taken away by this prayer to manifest and leave me. I command the spirits of drug addiction, fear, distrust, envy, murder, control, physical abuse, frozen psychic, demonic independence, mental weakness, lynching spirit, vigilante spirit and related spirits to go by the authority invested in me by being a Christian.

WALLS OF ARGUMENT PRAYER

I forgive black men, black women and black youth for the way they have treated me. Forgive me for the way I have treated them.

Deliverance

I command the spirits of distrust, meanness, spitefulness, physical abuse, unfaithfulness, control, disobedience, adultery, fornication, drug addiction, alcoholism, murder, hate, horoscopes, Eastern Star, Islam, hypocrisy, and Masonry to manifest and leave me.

List Of Demons
(Ministering Deliverance Within The Context Of The African American Experience)

Sins / Curses / Demons

Deuteronomy 27 and 28
Leviticus 26:40

Various Demons

Evil soul ties, sins of ancestors; **false self-respect, power, dignity and confidence**; word curses, desire for ungodly power and control, lack of family commitment or commitment to relationships, failure to thrive, forced submissiveness, loss of sons, blind justice, unworthiness, son of Belial, lack of peace, drive by killings, prison bars, slave labor, prejudice, racism, divorce, misplaced and misguided desires, drug sales, poor responsibility and accountability, emotional hurricane, deep sorrow, souls for sale, false prosperity, lack of trust, betrayal, invisibility, pretty children, gold dust, tradition, gambling spirit, divorce, broken marriages, families in rebellion, intimidation, unsaved children and teenagers, loneliness, rejection from the main steam culture, rejection from our spouses, wicked thoughts, stealing others' reputations, coveting, slander, gossip, maliciousness, unholy affections. Hurt, sorrow, racist, ungodliness, oppression, temper outburst, refusal behaviors, disgust, failure, beating, lynching, abandonment, loneliness, self-destruction, multiple personalities, double mindedness, schizophrenia, disassociation, pride (Leviathan, strength in his neck), lack of ability to give or receive love, animal spirits, aggression, hollowness, hunger, abduction, kidnap, unbelief, unproductiveness, rage, self-serving spirits, deception, ugly spirit, arrogance, vain imaginations, fits of rage, acrimony, unpleasantness, sullenness, animosity, hostility, provocation, vexation, grief, sorrow, upheaval, insurgence, mutiny, revolution, contentiousness, disputing, stubborn-headed, rebellious attitude against GOD, defiance, accepts no correction, provoking rejection, stiff-nakedness, overthrowing, destructive, convulsive, resistive, interfering, friction withstanding, repulsiveness, aggression, daring, scornfulness, confusion, division, ridicule, tension, hurt, insults, frustration, disgust, insecurity, difficulty learning, discord, selfishness, doubt, inability to achieve, fake sickness, hypochondriacs, domination

Sex

Rape, birthing illegitimate children, teen pregnancy, prostitution, men sharing, women sharing, low morals, lust not love, barrenness, bastard, flirting, sexual sin, abortions, sexual abuse of children, perversion, homosexuality, seduction, fornication, abuse and rape of women, power in the penis (Behemoth, strength in his loins), sexual promiscuity, adultery, fornication, incest, lust, sodomy, pornography, lesbianism, sex toys, oral sex, anal sex, bestiality

Infirmity
Infirmity, high blood pressure, heart disease, arthritis, lupus, cancer, stroke, hardening of arteries, mental illness, worry, pandemonium, anxiety, pharmakeia

Death
Death, destruction, Abaddon, Apollyon, suicide, abortion, murder and other crimes, death sentence, early death

Religion
False doctrine, abuse of scripture; **false prophesy, wealth or prosperity**; spiritual status, false prestige, preacher's whoop / squall, smooth talking, power of persuasion, domination, manipulation and control, straddling the fence, charmer, spiritual ambitious, lack of accountability, compromise, cover-up, attitude of superiority, verbal and physical abuse, spiritual weakness, vain arguments, profane fictions, abuse of titles, silly myths, irreverent babble, Godless chatter, demonic intercessory prayers, Rastafarianism, village shrine rituals, worship and open relationship with the dead, Orisa Worship (Yoruba), Voodoo (Vodun), ancestor reverence and worship, Religion (magic and healing), spiritualism, witchcraft, nature worship, incense burning, psychic prayers, spirit possession, abuse by men of the cloth, idolatry, Islam, church splits

Addictions
Addictions (drugs, cigarettes, alcohol, prescription drugs, gambling, excessive spending), self-destruction through use of substances to hide pain, obesity (overweight, love for food, gluttony, overeating, I'm Fat spirit)

Slavery
Slavery, spirits of fear, distrust, envy, murder, control, physical abuse, frozen psychic, demonic independence, mental weakness, lynching spirit, vigilante spirit and related spirits.

Black Interaction
spirits of distrust, meanness, spitefulness, physical abuse, unfaithfulness, control, disobedience, adultery, fornication, drug addiction, alcoholism, murder, hate, horoscopes, Eastern Star, Islam, hypocrisy and Masonry.

Occult
roots, Dr. Buzzard, oils (potions, powders, incense), dream books, numerology and other forms of divination, **black, white and candle magic,** dreams, incantation, superstition, occult, Herbal Medicine, divination, sorcery, mediumship, necromancy, kinship and royal rituals, ancestral intervention, reincarnation

Black
Down playing or hatred of African features (hair, nose, mouth, skin color), black hatred, hatred for Whites, darkie, blackie, Black pride, African pride, unlawful transfer of property belonging to Blacks, lack of inheritance, poverty

Demonic Tongues
Tongue of strange woman and of the serpent, viper's, flattering, smooth, slandering, deceitful, sharp, proud, lying, false, backbiting, stammering, crafty, confused, striving, devises mischief, full of adder's poison, froward, naughty, perverse, evil fire, double, **full of trouble, sin, mischief and iniquity**

Matriarchal
Matriarchal hierarchy due to absence of men in spirit and/or body, matriarchal headed homes, absent fathers, improper family structure, improper male / female relationships, improper alignment, Jezebel and Ahab spirits

CURSING OTHERS AND BEING CURSED
Prayer
Father, we want to bless others and be blessed rather than to curse others and be cursed. Please make us a blessing and take away the curse. We will get rid of cursed objects in our possession. We ask that you, other people and our descendents forgive us for anything we have done to bring the curse. We forgive our ancestors and others that have placed curses on us. Please forgive these people for psychic prayers, spoken curses, ancestral curses, parental curses, cursing by others, cursing ourselves, cursing our descendents, disobedience, Ahab and Jezebel, charismatic witchcraft, conceiving bastards, having incest, Indian curses, and other curse known or unknown that is found in THE HOLY WORD OF GOD.

I now break curses placed on me or my descendents. I break the curses back to ten generations or even to Adam and Eve on both sides of my family, and destroy legal holds and legal grounds that demons have to work in my life. I break curses that follow:

List Of Demons
Call out the demons that come in through the curses also.

Pestilence	Idol Worship	Graven Images
Consumption	Bastard	Pride
Fever	Wicked Balances	Catholic Prayers
Inflammation	Dislike/Hatred/Murder	Prince of Southern Curses
Extreme Burning	Curse of the Law	Prince of Occult
Blasting	Bless You Spirits	Witchcraft Curses
Mildew	Incest	Voodoo Curses
Botch of Egypt	Lesbians	Occult Curses
Emerods	Necromancers	American Indian Curses
Scab	Blaspheming	Charismatic Witchcraft
Itch	Sodomy	Horoscopes
Madness	Oral & Anal Sex	Rebellion

Blindness	Slackness	False Prophets
Astonishment of Heart	Deeper Teachings	Seances
Plagues	Irish Shamrock Hex	Fortune Telling
Sore Sicknesses	Fertility	Nonproductivity
Diseases of Egypt	Deceiving	Personal Poverty
Trembling of Heart	Adultery	Misrepresentation
Failing of Eyes	Disobedience	Perversion of Judgment
Sorrow of Mind	Cursed Objects	Doubt
Broken Vows	Thievery	Homosexual
Unicorn	False Swearing	Tulip
Twelve Petal Rosette	The Distlefink	Your Lucky Stars
Love & Romance	Eight Pointed Star	Friendship Hex
Pentacle/Pentagram	Eastern Star	Hexagram
Star of David	Mogen David	Cabalistic Magic Symbol
White Magic	Masonic Symbols	Freemasonry
Italian Horn	Leprechaun's Staff	Unicorn's Horn
Egyptian Ankh	Egyptian Sun God RA	Zodiac
Mexican Sun God	Buddhas	Crescent Moon & Star

Cursing, Vexation, Rebuke, Destroying, Perishing, Consuming, Groping
Not Prosper, Oppressed, Spoiled, Failure, Crushed, Smite, Pursuing
Sore Botch of Knees, Legs and Whole Body
Overtaking, Distress, Plucked, Chastisement, Removed, Not Healed
Astonishment, Proverb, Byword, Want, Besiege, Straitness, Evil

Emotionalism, Love of Money, Psychic Prayers, Idol Worship, Conceived in Lust, Abortion, Rejection, Physical Abuse, Emotional Abuse, Sexual Abuse, Bastard, Incest, Fornication, Strife, Alienation, Sickness, Deceit, Delusions, Cruelty, Lying, Seduction, Death, Troubling, Confusion, Lethargy, Misery, Destruction, Ignorance, Sorrow, Wickedness, Badness, Adversity, Affliction, Calamity, Displeasure, Distress, Grief, Harm, Hurt, Mischief, Sadness, Trouble, Vex, Wretchedness, Wrong, Perishing, Decay, Ruin, Corruptness, Destroying, Falling, Deluded, Allured, Enticed, Persuaded, Slumber, Stupor, Hardening, Error, Taking GOD's GLORY, Following Man, Witchcraft, Indian Spirits

ARE YOU LIVING WITH A CURSE?
Commands
I take authority over curses and their existence back to the tenth generation. I command that they be obliterated, erased, eradicated and reversed never to return to me again. I command that my body affected by curses go back into perfect order as GOD made it.

CURSES FOR SHEDDING INNOCENT BLOOD
Prayer
Dear Father in Heaven, there are curses that fall on individuals, families, races and nations for the sin of shedding innocent blood. This is a curse that travels down the

family line. I ask for forgiveness for myself and those before me who have sinned against you and others by shedding innocent blood.

We have greatly erred in shedding innocent blood in the United States. Forgive us of this terrible sin, redeem us from quilt and cleanse the land.

I repent of having become involved in acts that show worship and obedience to the Devil and his demons. I repent of occult acts: worship, drugs, sex, thievery, murder, etc. I break soul ties with others that I practiced these acts with.

You have given us power over the power of the Devil. I break the curse of shedding innocent blood off my family and my descendents. I break curses of idol worship, Satanism and illicit sex.

You have said that if I call on You, I can be delivered. I thank you for what you have done for me. I commit my life to you in a greater way than I have before. Please instruct me, help me to correct my life and bring it into subjection to You.

List Of Demons

We cast out demons associated with shedding innocent blood, murder of innocent people, sacrificing children to demons, idols of sex, spirits of anger, sadness, dejection, rage, hate, envy, jealousy, pretense, falseness, bribery, lying, killing, rebellion, **Jezebel and Ahab**, greed, pride, cursing, deceit, fraud, oppression, **Baal and sexual idols**, lust, **occult, illicit drugs and sex**, seeking forbidden knowledge, burning incense, worship of sex, terror, cowardliness, idolatry, witchcraft, thievery, murder, Satanism, **Asmodeous and marriage breaking spirits**, and related demonic families.

HOUSE CURSES
Cleaning Your House Prayer

I come to you about cursed objects and demon infestation in my possessions and home, and in me. I forgive my ancestors, descendants and others who have had spiritual influence over me. I ask you to forgive and bless them, especially with salvation. Please forgive me and I forgive myself for spiritual adultery. I forgive those who have cursed me; forgive me for cursing others. I break the curses and demonic soul ties including psychic and Catholic prayers. I will clean out my house of cursed objects or exorcise objects that I don't own. I will anoint my house with oil and drive the evil spirits out of the house. Show me cursed objects, demon infestation and spirits that need to be cast out of people.

CURSE OF PRIDE
Prayer

I come to you in the matter of pride. Pride is an abomination to you. I renounce pride and turn away from it. I humble myself before you and come to you as a little child. I ask you to forgive me and I forgive myself. I do this for sins committed in pride that would have affected me.

I forgive my ancestors, descendents, and anyone else that has had spiritual or carnal authority over me. I ask that you save them, bless them with spiritual blessings, bring them into truth and meet their needs out of your riches in glory.

List Of Demons

Leviathan, King of the Children of Pride: (Job 41 and 104:16; Isa. 27:1) Using logic rather than being led by GOD; carnal justification to know the things of GOD; hinders spiritual growth; disturbs concentration in Bible study and prayer; weariness and sleepiness in worship services; and blocks mind. Causes pride, mourning, spiritual darkness, arrogance, spiritual pride, ego, little pride, rationalization, distracts, brooding, melancholy, depression, gloominess, mental dejection, irascibility, mourning, spiritual darkness, arrogance, ego.

Rahab: dragon, pride, **(Isa. 51:9-10)**.

Orion: compromise of THE WORD OF GOD, counterfeit gifts, false peace, piety.

Prince Charming: intellectual and philosophical spirits, religious spirits, false gifts, veneer of spirituality.

Absalom: pride, vanity, rebellion, deception, seduction, treachery: mind idolatry, vanity, perfection, competition, schizophrenia, self righteousness, haughtiness, importance, arrogance, self deception, ego.

Mind Idolatry: pride, intellectualism, rationalization, ego.

Vanity: Belphegar, Belfagar, Apollyon, Scorpion, fears, Absalom, pride, Orion, perfection, schizophrenia.

Perfectionism: pride, vanity, frustration, irritability, intolerance, anger, criticism, schizophrenia.

Competition: pride, driving, argument, ego, compromise, indecision, blocked spiritual growth, Orion.

Schizophrenia: pride, etc.

Ego: mind idolatry, pride, perfection, competition, schizophrenia.

Carvar: spiritual destruction, under spirit of Lucifer.

Carbar: a ruler: spiritual blockage, blocks spiritual truth.

Reserpcarian, Rucipacerian, a controller: spirit and will, blocks spirit and will.

Additimus: blocks spiritual truth.

Markai, Markiah: blocks spiritual understanding, causes spiritual blindness.

Morondo: blocks reading of The Word, blocks spiritual light.

Remus, Remur: causes sleep in spiritual environment.

(See Self Righteousness, Haughtiness, Importance, Arrogance, Self Deception.)

CURSE OF AHAB AND JEZEBEL
Prayer

I ask you to forgive me and I forgive my ancestors for being Jezebels and Ahabs. Please forgive me for idol worship, passivity, irresponsibility, fear, weakness, sexual impurity, pride, selfishness, witchcraft, control, criticism, jealousy, rebellion, competition, retaliation, marriage breaking, child abuse and worshiping other Gods. I command the spirits to manifest, identify and reveal themselves. I command the families of demons to come out as your name is called.

Ahab And Jezebel Demons Short List

Ahab Demons:

Ahab
Abdicating Leadership
Adultery
Aggression
Angry
Bitterness
Communication breakdown
Conditional love
Childish behavior
Competition
Covetousness
Compromise
Clashing conflict
Considering GOD's things trivial
Call evil good - good, evil
Displeased
Disobedient
Dirty stories
Degradation
Destruction of family priesthood
Doubting manhood
Drunkenness
Emasculations
Emotional cripple
Failure
Fearful
Fear of getting hurt
Fear of women
Filth
Following sins of the father
God of Sports
God of Jobs
Heavy spirited
Hatred of women
Homosexuality
Hurts

Idol Worship
Impotence
Joblessness
Laziness

Lust
Lust of material things
Lack of confidence
Liking sensual women
Macho spirit
Misunderstandings
Manipulating women
Murder
No order
No peace
No unity
Overloading wife
Pride
Pornography
Pouting
Passive quitter
Rebellious children
Rejection
Resentment
Scared
Separation & divorce
Sibling rivalry
Sluggishness
Stoicism
Tragic mistakes
Unemotional
Upset children
Workaholic

Inability to designate authority
Leaving things of GOD to wife
Worship of enterprise, success, profit, promotion & wealth

Jezebel Demons:

Accusation
Aggression

Indecision
Intimidation

Attention seeking	Insinuation
Arrogance	Insecurity
Beguiling	Inadequate
Belittling	Intellectualism
Bickering	Inhospitable
Backbiting	Interference
Brash, bossy woman	Jealousy
Bedroom blackmail	Jezebel
Conniving	Lack of confidence
Contention	Lying
Continuous complaining	Lawlessness
Condemnation	Laziness
Confusion	Manipulation
Counterfeit spiritual gifts	Mistrust
Conditional love	Nagging
Charming	Overindulgence
Controlling spirits	Pouting
Dissatisfaction	Pride
Demands	
Double Mindedness	Psychology
Doubt	Philosophy
Disunity	Projected guilt
Discord	Quick temper
Disruption	Retaliation
Distrust	Revenger
Deception	Rationalization
Delusion	Rebellion
Demanding	Strife
Defeat	Slander
Determined maneuvers	Sharp temper
Dominance	Short temper
Emotional outburst	Sorcery
Failure	
Fear	Sensitive
Frustration	Sharp tongue
Forsaking protection	Sleepiness
Female dominance & control	Shame
Female hardness	Suicide
Fierce determination	Spiritual blindness
False sickness	Self-defeating
Finger pointing	Sorrow
Frigidity	Turmoil
Grief	Ungodly discipline
Hatred of men	Unbelief
Hot temper	Ugliness
Hasty marriage	Vanity

Hopelessness
Hypnotic control
Inability to give or receive love
Irresponsibility

Perversion (sexual & spiritual)
Shirking responsibilities

Whining
Witchcraft
Worldly wisdom

Ahab And Jezebel Demons Long List
Ahab Demons

Son Of Jezebel
Son Of Ahab
Father of Jezebel
Father of Ahab

Passivity
Laziness
Inertia
Lethargy
Sloth
Indolent
Inactivity
Avoiding Work
I Hate Working
Don't Want To Work

Irresponsibility
Unreliability
Childishness
Pouting
Temper Tantrums
Lassitude
Undependability
Carelessness
Ineptitude
Foolishness
Little Boy
Mama's Boy
Good Old Boy
Emasculation

Fear
Of Responsibility
Of Authority
Of Rebuke
Of Ridicule
Of Failing
Blaming Wife
Blaming Others

Weakness
Insecurity
Indecision
Compromise
Lack Of Character
Lack Of Authority
Leaning On Wife
Leaning On Others
Milque-Toast

Sexual Impurity
Impotence
Homosexuality
Effeminate
Succubus
(For additional demons, see Jezebel list.)

Names Of The Gods

Baal	Perseus	Tammuz
Baalim	Phoroneus	Lord Of Heaven
Bel	Nimrod	The Sun
Belial	Nin	Belus

Merodach
Osiris
Horus
Apis
Saurun
Baal-Berith
Baal-Zebub
Baal-Sutekh
El-Berith
Lord Of The Flies
Kronos (Bread Of Life)
Nin
Ninus
Dyonisius
Bacchus
Iacchus
Siva, Shiva
Moloch

Ahab: If you have cast out the previous demons, cast Ahab out now. The names of **Sexual Impurity** demons are essentially the same for Jezebel and Ahab with the exception of female or male demons.)

Jezebel Demons

Daughter of Jezebel
Daughter of Ahab
Mother of Jezebel
Mother of Ahab

Sexual Impurity
Lust
Fantasy Lust
Defilement
Adultery
Fornication
Incest
Exposure
Frigidity
Smut
Filth
Oral Sex
Anal Sex
Sodomy
Take Me
Rape
Obscenity
Pornography
Child Pornography
Child Molestation
Pornographic Flashbacks
Pornographic Memory
Burning Passion
Harlotry
Prostitution
Sexual Incitement
Sexual Enticement
Lesbianism
Homosexuality
Bi-Sexual
Cross Dresser
Transvestite
Exhibitionism
Flirting
Lust of the Eyes

Pride
Haughtiness
Ego
Self
Egotism
Conceit
Vanity
Self-Righteousness
Self-Importance, The Queen
Arrogance
Center of Attention
Superiority
Pride of Life
Self-Sufficiency
Pretension

Selfishness
Egoism
Egotism
Egocentric
Egomania
Number One
Self-Centered
Self-Obsessed
Self-Idolatry
Self-Admiration
Self-Approval
Self-Interest
Self-Concern
Self-Seeker
Taker, not Giver
People User
Inconsiderate
Narcissistic
Abortion

Lust of the Flesh
Inordinate Affection
Nymphomania
Masturbation
Sadism
Masochism
Dominatrix
Satyrism
Seduction
Sensuality
 Incubus
Perversity
Perverse Spirit
Cupid
Eros

Witchcraft
Charismatic Witchcraft
White Magic
Black Magic
Sorcery
Fortune Telling
Horoscopes
Astrology
Tarot Cards
Crystal Ball
ESP
Mind Control
Conjurations
Incantations
Potions
Burning Of Dedicated Candles
Channeling
Crystals
Wicca
Satanism
Charms
Fetishes
Levitation
Palmistry
Handwriting Analysis
Hair Reading
Iridiology
Automatic Handwriting
Ouija Board
Pendulum

Child Abuse
Child Neglect
Child Abandonment
Child Murderer

Control
Possessiveness
Dominance
Deception
Ascendancy
Lying
Manipulation
Scheming
Strategy
String-Pulling
Wire-Pulling
Do It My Way
Authoritarian
Tyrannical
Argumentative
Upper Hand
Whip Hand
Ruler
Master
Revenge

Criticism
Critical Spirit
Judgmental, Judging
Accusation
Fault-Finding
Censure
Prejudice

Jealousy
Envy
Suspicion
Distrust
Covetousness
Greed
Discontent

Rebellion
Willfulness
Disobedience
Anti-Submissiveness

Divination
Enchantment
Fire Gazing
Astral Projection
Kabala
Hypnosis
Medium
Psychic Powers
Psychokinesis
Telepathy
Table Tipping
Talismans
Fetishes
Santeria
Voodoo
The Witch
Poltergeist
Tea Leaf Reading
Palmistry
Curses
Hexes
Vexes

Retaliation
Destruction
Spite
Hatred
Malice
Treachery

Marriage-Breaking
Hatred Of Husband
Despising Husband
Belittling
Lack Of Intimacy
Arguing
Contentious
Anti-Submissiveness
Distance
Separation
Divorce
Asmodeus
Osmodeus
Matrimonial Discord
Never Satisfied

Stubbornness
Defiance
Opposition
Resistance
Obstinacy

Competition
I'm Better Than You
I Am The Best
I Win
What I Think Is The Way It Is
What I Say Is The Way It Is
I Have The Last Word
I Am More Important
My Choices Are The Best
I Go In First
I Know Better
Competitive
Arguing
Driving
Pride
Ego
Headstrong
Intimidating
Strife
Contention
Disagreement
Debate
Altercation
Quarreling
Discussion
Controvert
Conflict
Dissension
Friction
Fighting
Battle
Clash
Combat
Dispute
Assert
Maintain
Insist

Names of Goddesses
Ashera

Child Abuse
Provocation

Disrespect Of Sons (or Daughters)
Belittlement Of Sons (or Daughters)
Humiliation Of Sons (or Daughters)
Hatred Of Sons (or Daughters)
Jealousy Of Sons (or Daughters)
Negligence Of Sons (or Daughters)
Destruction Of Sons (or Daughters)

Physical Abuse
Mental Abuse
Emotional Abuse
Psychological Abuse
Verbal Abuse
Sexual Abuse
Incest Abortion
Murder
Moloch

Goddesses Of The Feminist Movement
Songi
Athena
Tara
Pasowee
Ishtar
Ixmucane
Adita
Nashe

Wiccan Goddesses
Artemis
Astarte
Athene
Dione
Melusine
Aphrodite
Cerridwen
Dana
Arianhod
Isis
Bride
Changing Woman
Shakti

Asherim
Ashtaroth

Ashtoreth
Athirat
Astarte
Astoreth Of The Sidonians
Ishtar
Goddess Of The Groves
Athirat
Asterie
Astrea
Themis
Virgin Themis
The Perfect One
Goddess Of Justice
Semiramis
Beltis
Queen Of Heaven
Eve
Aphrodite
Mylitta
The Mediatrix
Woman Mediator
Melitza
Melissa
Rhea
Cybele
Melitta
Venus
Archia
Arkh
Diana
Diana Of The Ephesians
Diana Of The Romans
Artemis
Moon Goddess
Ash-Toret

Semiramis
Immaculately Conceived
Blessed Virgin Mary
Aida Odeo
Beltis
Goddess Of Wisdom
Anahita
Ardvi Sura Anahita
Anat
Anath
Atargatis
Isis
Ceres
Shing-Moo
Sati
Virgin Mary
Re-Anen
Josephine
Delilah
St. Barbara
Aida-Odeo
Mother Of The Gods
Mother Of Lies
Mother Of Cheating
Inanna
Enheduanna
Gaia
Hather
Demeter
Kali
Ariadne

Ash-Turit
Mother Of The Gods
Minerva
Athena

Jezebel: If you have cast out the previous demons, cast out Jezebel now. Although Delilah, Eve and Josephine are not Goddesses, they have been added because they are found as demons among the demons of the Goddesses. I believe Josephine refers to the wife of Napoleon.

SECTION 4 - WORD CURSES

CONTENTS
1. **OVERALL CURSES**
    1. Scripture
    2. Scripture For Victorious Living
    3. Preface
    4. All Curses
    5. Sources Of Curses
        1. God
        2. Ourselves
    6. Six Steps To Freedom From Curses
    7. Curses On Children
    8. Prayer For Biblical Curses
2. **CLEANING YOUR HOUSE**
    1. Prayer
3. **CURSING OTHERS AND BEING CURSED**
    1. Spoken Curses
    2. Ancestral Curses
    3. Parental Curses
    4. Cursing By People Other Than Your Ancestors
    5. Cursing Yourself
    6. Origin Of Curses
    7. The Curse Of Charismatic Witchcraft
    8. Prayer
4. **PSYCHIC PRAYERS**
    1. Testimony
5. **CHRISTIAN FANTASY (LIES NOT TRUTH)**
    1. Preface
    2. Definitions
    3. Lies
    4. Christian Fables And Cliches
        1. Untruths
        2. Truths
    5. Prophecy Myths
    6. General Myths
    7. Prayer Before Deliverance
6. **LIES, DECEIT AND FLATTERY**
    1. The Little White Lie
    2. Evangelistically Speaking
    3. The Deliberate Lie
    4. Flattery
    5. Pretending
    6. Deceit And Deception
    7. Falseness

8. Cheating
9. Dishonesty
10. Responsibility Of A Minister
11. Prayer
12. List Of Demons
    1. Christian Fantasy - Lies Not Truth
    2. Lies, Deceit And Flattery
    3. Bad Habits Of Thinking And Reacting

OVERALL CURSES
Scripture

Deut. 28:1-2 And it shall come to pass, if thou shalt (shalt not) **hearken diligently unto the voice of the Lord thy God, to observe and to do all his commandments which I command thee this day, that the Lord thy God will set** (not set) **thee on high above all nations of the earth: and all these blessings shall** (shall not) **come on thee, and overtake thee, if thou shalt** (shalt not) **hearken unto the voice of the Lord thy God.** (Read it both with and without.)

Deut. 28:15 But it shall come to pass, if thou wilt not hearken unto the voice of the Lord thy God, to observe to do all His commandments and His statutes which I command thee this day; that all these curses shall come upon thee, and overtake thee. (Obey or be cursed!)

Psa. 39:1 I will take heed to my ways, **that I sin not with my tongue:** I will keep my mouth with a bridle. (Do not sin with your mouth.)

Prov. 6:2 Thou art snared with the words of thy mouth, thou are taken with the words of thy mouth. (You are snared by your words.)

Prov. 18:21 Death and life are in the power of the tongue: and they that love it shall eat the fruit thereof. (You speak death or life.)

Prov. 23:7 For as he thinketh in his heart, so is he: Eat and Drink, saith he to thee; but his heart is not with thee. (You are as you think.)

Prov. 26:2 As the bird by wandering, as the swallow by flying, so the curse causeless shall not come. (There must be sin in your life.)

Ecc. 10:20 Curse not the king, no not in thy thought; and curse not the rich in thy bed chamber: for a bird of the air shall carry the voice, and that which hath wings shall tell the matter. (This is probably a demon.)

Isaiah 3:12 As for my people, children are their oppressors, and women rule over them. O my people, they which lead thee cause thee to err, and destroy the way of thy paths. (This is a family out of divine order who are cursing each other.)

Isa. 41:10 Fear thou not; for I am with thee; be not dismayed; for I am thy God: I will strengthen thee; yea, I will help thee; yea, I will uphold thee with the right hand of my righteousness. (Do not fear others.)

Matt. 12:37 By thy words thou shalt be justified, **and by they words thou shalt be condemned.** (You condemn yourself.)

II Cor. 4:8-10 We are troubled on every side, yet not distressed; we are perplexed, **but not in despair;** persecuted, **but not forsaken;** cast down, **but not destroyed;** always bearing about in the body the dying of the Lord Jesus, that the life also of Jesus might be manifest in our body. (We are troubled, perplexed, persecuted, cast down and crucified with Christ.)

Eph. 4:29 Let no corrupt communication proceed out of your mouth, but that which is good to the **use of edifying,** that it may minister grace unto the hearers. (Do not use corrupt language.)

I Tim. 6:10 For the love of money is the root of all evil: which while some coveted after, they have erred from the faith, and pierced themselves through with many sorrows. (If you love money, you will have many curses.)

Heb. 10:35-36 Cast not away therefore your confidence, which hath great recompense of reward. For ye have need of patience, that, after ye have done the will of God, ye might receive the promise. (Have confidence and patience.)

Rev. 12:10 And I heard a loud voice saying in heaven, Now is come salvation, and strength, and the kingdom of our God, and the power of his Christ: **for the accuser of our brethren** is cast down, which accused them before our God day and night.

Scripture For Victorious Living

I Sam. 17:44 And I will smite thee, and take thine head from thee.
Neh. 8:10 The joy of the Lord is my strength.
Psa. 37:23 The steps of a good man are ordered by the Lord.
Psa. 46:10 Be still and know that I am God.
Psa. 91:15 He shall call upon me, and I will answer him; I will be with him in trouble; I will deliver him, and honor him.
Psa. 103:3 He healeth all thy diseases.
Psa. 118:24 This is the day which the Lord hath made; I will rejoice and be glad in it.
Psa. 141:3 Set a watch, O Lord, before my mouth; keep the door of my lips.
Prov. 4:23 Keep thy heart with all diligence; for out of it are the issues of life.
Isa. 30:15 In quietness and in confidence (faith) shall be your strength.
Isa. 43:2 When thou passest through the water, I will be with thee; and through the river, they shall not overflow thee: when thou walkest through the fire, thou shalt not be burned; neither shall the flame kindle upon thee.
Matt. 12:34 For out of the abundance of the heart the mouth speaketh.
Matt. 17:20 If ye have faith as a grain of mustard seed, nothing shall be impossible unto you.
Mark 9:23 If thou canst believe, all things are possible to him that believeth.
Mark 11:24 What things soever ye desire, when ye pray, believe that ye receive them, and ye shall have them.
Mark 16:17-18 They shall take up serpents; and if they drink any deadly thing, it shall not hurt them; they shall lay hands on the sick, and they shall recover.
Luke 10:19 Power over all the power of the enemy.
John 14:12 He that believeth on me, the works that I do shall he do also; and greater works than these shall he do.
Rom. 2:11 No respect of persons.
Rom. 8:28 We know that all things work together for good to them that love God, to them who are the called according to his purpose.
Rom. 8:37 We are more than conquerors through him that loved us.
Rom. 10:10 For with the heart man believeth unto righteousness; and with the mouth confession is made unto salvation.
Rom. 12:2 Be ye transformed **by the renewing of your mind.**
I Cor. 3:21-22 All things are yours: whether the world, or life, or death, or things present, or things to come.
II Cor. 5:17 If any man be in Christ, he is a new creature: old things are passed away; behold, all things are become new.
Phil. 4:13 I can do all things through Christ which strengtheneth me.
Heb. 11:1 Faith is the evidence of things not seen.

James 5:15 The prayer of faith shall heal the sick.
I Peter 2:24 By Jesus' stripes ye were healed.

Preface
This lesson will look at curses overall and cover a lot of areas where we can receive curses. The effects can be many in our spirit, soul and body. You could say in our spiritual, mental, physical and material lives. Curses come from our nation, ancestors, ourselves, descendents, and others, or anyone or anything that can affect us spiritually.

A person who **confesses** fear, anxiety, sickness, and defeat does so because he **believes** in fear, anxiety, sickness, and defeat! We must **stop** thinking and expecting sickness, poverty, inability, and failure. **If ye have faith as a grain of mustard seed, nothing shall be impossible unto you.**

Are You Living With A Curse?
A curse is uttering a wish of evil against one; to imprecate evil; to call for mischief or injury to fall upon; to execrate, to bring evil upon or to; to blast, vex, harass or torment with great calamities.

All Curses
We are told to keep all the words of the Holy Bible. GOD is serious about us obeying His inspired WORD OF GOD. For every verse in THE HOLY BIBLE that you obey, you are blessed. For every verse in THE HOLY BIBLE that you disobey, you are cursed.

Sources Of Curses
There are many sources of curses. Basically there are five main sources of curses: nationality, bloodline, others, GOD and ourselves.

God
The main source of curses is disobeying THE BIBLE.

Ourselves
1. Having **cursed words** (written or spoken) in our home or possessions.
2. **Ourselves** when we curse others.
3. **Agreement with shedding innocent blood** such as abortion.
4. Having **cursed thoughts**.

Six Steps To Freedom From Curses
It is more effective if you work on specific rather than general curses:

1. **Identify the names** of the curses and the sins that caused the curses.
2. **Forgive** those that caused the curses for their sins against God in placing these curses on the family line.
3. **Repent and pray** to God to take away the right for the curses to be in your lives.
4. **Break the curses** in the Name of Jesus Christ.
5. **Cast out the demons** that came in with the curses.

6. **Discipline your life** and sin no more.

Curses On Children
1. Curse of idol worship extends to **fourth generation** of great grandchildren (Exodus 20:1-5).
2. Children who curse their parents (Exodus 21:17).

Prayer For Biblical Curses
In the Name of Jesus Christ, I forgive my ancestors and anyone else that has cursed me. I ask God to forgive them and me. I break curses placed on me and my descendants. I break the curses back to ten generations or even to Adam and Eve on both sides of my family. I destroy legal holds and legal grounds that demons have to work in my life.

I rebuke, break, loose myself and my children from evil curses, charms, vexes, hexes, spells, jinxes, psychic powers, bewitchment, witchcraft and sorcery that have been put upon me or my family line from persons, occult or psychic sources. I break these curses in The Name of Jesus Christ. I cancel connected or related spirits and command them to leave me. I thank you, Lord, for setting me free. Amen.

CLEANING YOUR HOUSE
Five Steps
It is more effective if you work on specific rather than general sins and cursed objects:

1. Five-way prayer of forgiveness - **you forgive your ancestors, descendants and others** (ask God to forgive and bless them). **Ask God to forgive you; you forgive yourself for sins against your body.**
2. Break curses and soul ties **from others and to others;** break curses of psychic or religious prayers.
3. Clean out house of those objects.
4. Anoint house with oil and drive evil spirits out of house.
5. Cast demons out of people that came in thru curses from objects.

Prayer
Father, I come to you about cursed objects and demon infestation in my possessions, home and me. I forgive my ancestors, descendants and others who have had spiritual influence over me. I ask you to forgive and bless them, especially with salvation. Please forgive me and I forgive myself for spiritual adultery. I forgive those who have cursed me; forgive me for cursing others. I break the curses and demonic soul ties including psychic and religious prayers. I will clean out my house of cursed objects. I will anoint my house with oil and drive the evil spirits out of the house. Show me spirits that need to be cast out of people. In Jesus Name I pray. Amen.

CURSING OTHERS AND BEING CURSED
Spoken Curses
We can pray a psychic prayer or we can speak against another person either in our thoughts or out loud. We need to be careful what we think and speak. The words we think or speak go out into the air and they have power to do good or evil.

Ancestral Curses
The first curses that we can receive are those placed on us by our ancestors which include our parents. We are innocent and have committed no sin but we still are cursed because of what those did who were in spiritual authority over us.

Parental Curses
The parents can curse the child in the womb, after the child is born and until it dies. **This is frightening when you think about the consequences of your actions on your children and grandchildren.**

Common examples of cursing the child in the womb include not wanting the child when it is conceived, and the way the child is talked to or thought about.

Common examples of cursing the child after it is born include rejecting the child in some manner, such as wanting a boy when a girl is born, and not quickly changing their minds, cursing the child in thought or words, and mistreating the child mentally, spiritually or emotionally.

Cursing By People Other Than Your Ancestors
You can be cursed by people other than your ancestors. These include those in the grip of the Devil: Satan worshipers, witches and warlocks, covens, fortune tellers and anyone practicing witchcraft. They include those in Christianity who would speak against you and pray psychic prayers for you.

How can you be cursed by these people? There must be a cause for the curse to land. I have not seen anyone that lives a blameless, sinless, perfect life according to the whole Word of God including myself.

Cursing Yourself
Other than being cursed by others, you can curse yourself.

Origin Of Curses
Curses come from God and are carried out by Satan with permission from God. **Curses can come to you from your ancestors or those who are not your relatives. You can curse yourself. Curses can go out from you to your descendents or to others not your relatives.**

The Curse Of Charismatic Witchcraft

Charismatic witchcraft is exercising control over other Christians. We have no right to control others! God gave us a free will and He will not try to control us! Therefore, we enter into agreement with Satan when we attempt to control others and we are practicing witchcraft!

Prayer

Father, we want to bless others and be blessed, rather than curse others and be cursed. Please make us a blessing and take away the curse. We will get rid of cursed objects in our possession. We ask that you, other people and our descendents forgive us for anything we have done by cursing ourselves, and cursing our descendents and others. We forgive our ancestors and others that have placed curses on us. Please forgive these people for psychic prayers, spoken curses, ancestral curses, parental curses, cursing by others, charismatic witchcraft and any other curse that is found in the Holy Word of God.

We break the curses back to ten generations or even to Adam and Eve on both sides of our families. We destroy legal holds and legal grounds that demons have to work in our lives. We do this in The Name Of Jesus Christ: Lord, Master and Savior.

PSYCHIC PRAYERS

A psychic prayer is any prayer that does not line up with the Word of God. If you pray contrary to the Bible, then you are not praying to God but to Satan. Satan then has the legal right before God to loose demons on the people that you prayed for as well as yourself. Psychic prayers are good ways to curse others and to be cursed in return.

Men are addressed as free agents and may be saved if they will. In other words, men and women have a free will to accept or reject the things of God. He gives them a free will and we have no right to violate their free will.

Testimony

This is a vivid testimony of a pastor, his wife and their church about what happened when psychic prayers were prayed for them.

This situation came about because the pastor taught the people about unforgiveness and entered into deliverance. The families would not forgive each other for past offenses. Some of the congregation did not want deliverance, and fled from the teaching and ministering of it.

After the people left the church, they went to other churches and prayer groups. There, they prayed for the pastor that God would make him get back into line and give up deliverance. **This is not a prayer to God but a prayer to Satan. Their prayers loosed demons on the pastor and his family.**

They were trying to control the pastor and his wife. These were Jezebels that wanted the church back like they had it before. They had controlled the church and the pastor whom they called **"Our Little Boy".**

The demons manifested and knocked the curtains off the wall of the pastor's home. One demon manifested and walked in front of our car as we were driving back home that night after this visit. The demon looked like a half man from the waist down. The purpose was to cause me to drive off the road and to kill us.

The Holy Spirit showed the pastor and his wife what had happened because of the psychic prayers. They forgave about eighty people that had prayed against them, broke the curses and soul ties, cast out the demons and sent them back to the senders, and prayed for the people to see what they were doing wrong.

Many things happened to the people that left and prayed against the church. They suffered from divorce, family problems, sickness and death. As you can see, it is dangerous to pray psychic prayers and fight against deliverance.

CHRISTIAN FANTASY
(LIES NOT TRUTH)
Preface
We frequently encounter Christian fantasy especially in the Full-Gospel Movement. There is much ignorance and many myths about Christianity, deliverance and warfare.

Definitions
Fantasy: hallucination, fanciful, imagination, caprice, unrealistic, improbable, daydream.
Fable: story, fictitious, legend, falsehood, lie.
Myth: parable, **tradition,** unfounded, false, imaginary, unverifyable.

Lies
Prov. 6:19 A false witness that speaketh lies. There are a lot of pat phrases in the Christian world that are not true when put to the test. This is false witness and deceives others.
Prov. 19:9 He that speaketh lies shall perish. It is dangerous to follow false teachings of any kind and you will perish in some degree. You will pay for any area of the Bible that you are ignorant of. Earline said that you burn while you learn.
Isa. 9:15 The prophet that teacheth lies, he is the tail. Instead of being a head of Christianity, he will be a tail.
Isa. 28:15 Under falsehood have we hid ourselves. Are Christian fables your refuge?
Jer. 14:14 The prophets prophesy lies in my name. People prophesy in the Name of God but the prophesy comes from their soul. It is a soulish prophesy that frequently ends with **thus saith the Lord.**
Jer. 23:25 Saying, I have dreamed, I have dreamed. These are false prophets with false dreams.
Jer. 23:32 Cause my people to err by their lies, and by their lightness. False prophesy will cause the people to err. Taking Christianity lightly is error.

I Tim. 4:2 Speaking lies in hypocrisy. Hypocrites who depart from the faith continue to teach lies.

Christian Fables And Cliches

There are many fables and cliches that are passed off as the Gospel. **Generally, these are sayings that make you feel good.** They take on many different forms. If repeated often enough, the Christian world believes they are true. Some of these fables and cliches follow; the list could go on and on.

Untruths

1. God will do everything for you; you don't have to do anything for yourself.
2. God will take care of your family if you take care of God's business.
3. All of God's promises are ours.

Truths

1. God will always do His part of the covenant; we must do our part also.
2. We have no right to neglect our families.
3. The promises are ours only if we meet the conditions. For every promise there is a condition.

Prophecy Myths

Prophecies can be a blessing or a curse. Personal prophecy has caused some Christians to try to make it come true with disastrous results. The most danger for abuse lies in personal prophecy. Charismatic witches use personal prophecy to control others. Some Christians think that they have to have a word from the Lord or there is something wrong with them.

The true prophet does not make any mistakes. All of his prophecies come true. In the Old Testament, if the prophet missed God, he was killed (Deut. 13:1-5, 18:20).

Many prophecies are soulish prophecies which are made up in the mind of man or woman. Frequently they do not line up with the Bible. Sometimes people prophecy just to be noticed.

You have a responsibility to check out everything you see, hear or read by the Word of God, by the Holy Spirit within you, and by your intelligence. Otherwise, you will follow every wind of false doctrine.

Some prophecy is divination. Divination is the false gift of prophecy. It has destroyed churches and ministries. The diviners want to take over the pastor and the church.

Satan has a counterfeit for everything that God has created. Just because it is spiritual and happens in the church, does not mean that it is from God. The demons go to church with the congregation to hinder or destroy the church.

General Myths

Earline was trying to be holy and asked God to take her thoughts. God told her "He wouldn't touch her thoughts with a ten-foot pole". Don't expect God to cleanse your mind; you have to do the work. God will help you to along the path of life.

The following are a few negative statements or myths:

There is a single answer to my problems and living the Christian life. My problems in life can be worked out overnight. We can pick and choose what parts of the Bible to follow. It is not necessary to discipline our soul or body. We can let our minds be blank and God will fill them. We do not have to take care of our body; God will heal us when we get sick. We can let others feed us spiritually; we don't need to do it ourselves. We don't need to go to church; all we have to do is watch television evangelism. If we don't like deliverance, we can ignore it. God will supply everything we desire. If we can just find an anointed man or woman of God, they will pray for us and everything will be fine. We can live with one foot in the world and one foot in the Kingdom of God. If you do God's work, you can ignore your responsibilities. I can be a passive Christian and watch others do the work of God. The pastor and leaders do the work, not me. I am not in a war; God will fight all of my battles. All I have to do is to follow my pastor; he will hear from God for me. We can live a sinful life and receive all of God's blessings. I can sin, get forgiven and my family will not suffer. All we need to have in the church is token deliverance. Rejection is not a demon. I have a right to my unforgiveness because of the way I have been treated. Sex is love. Bad emotions are not demonic. I do not have to examine every area of my life. I can keep my cursed objects without causing any harm.

We can get all of our demons cast out in one grand event. I can be ashamed of my deliverance; God won't mind. When someone makes me mad, I can react however I feel. I can be ignorant of Satan's wiles; what I don't know can't hurt me. God is love; He won't send me to Hell. I can do anything I want to; God will protect me. God is pie-in-the-sky by-and-by. I do not need to get my demons cast out; all I need is to get prayer for me to be healed. It is all right to take mind control drugs. I need to go to a psychiatrist; God is not interested in my mind. The sins of my ancestors will not cause me any problems. I can do things my way; God will approve.

Prayer Before Deliverance

I forgive those who have controlled me with charismatic witchcraft. Please forgive me for practicing witchcraft and trying to control other people's wills. I ask God to forgive me. I take authority over these evil forces, break evil soul ties and break curses placed on me. I command these spirits to come out of me in The Name Of Jesus Christ.

LIES, DECEIT AND FLATTERY
The Little White Lie

How many Christians feel that they can tell a little white lie and it will not hurt anyone? What damage could it cause you and those related to you: Christian family and blood-related family? Since we are the Body of Christ and every Christian is related to every other Christian, then what we do affects everyone else. Every lie gives Satan an opportunity to use it against you, the person you told the lie to, and the Body of Christ.

Why not tell the truth in love? If you truly love that person, you will tell them the truth. If you are after some selfish gain, you will not be truthful with that person so that they will feel good about you. God tells us the truth to help us; Satan tells us a lie to hurt us.

Evangelistically Speaking

This is a term used by ministers to talk about their meetings, church or congregation. They exaggerate the numbers to make them look good to other ministers and Christians. These are white lies.

The Deliberate Lie

When a Christian tells a deliberate lie, they are really opening themselves up to a demonic attack. They fully know it is a lie, but they deliberately go ahead and tell it anyway.

The Bible describes these people as liars:
You could say your father is the Devil because he is the father of lies. Just like him, your part will be in the Lake of Fire and Brimstone; you shall not escape and shall perish.

Liars are failures, use bad tactics, a sword is upon them, are deceivers, have naughty tongues, poor men are better, commit perjury in the spiritual world, the truth is not in them, set a trap for themselves, do not respect themselves, delight in lies, are false witnesses, make lies their refuge, lie to God's people, cause themselves to make mistakes, will eat the fruit of their lies, think-up lies, teach and prophesy lies, trust in lies, are weary with lies, are an abomination to God, are recognized as liars, do not walk in the Spirit, are false, lie to God, walk in darkness and speak in hypocrisy.

Flattery

You are trying to deceive the person by being insincere and praising the person without justification. You see a lot of flattery in the world. You expect it in the carnal world where people are trying to advance their cause.

Why are Christian laymen and ministers so weak that they need to be praised just to do their jobs? Why do pastors have to build themselves up and have their congregations build them up? Why do people try to get the Glory that belongs to God?

Pretending

Pretending is another form of lying. You could use names of demons like affectation, theatrics, playacting, sophistication and pretension.

You put on your Sunday go-to-meeting clothes and artificial face. This is your facade to show the world that you are a good Christian. You may act like the Devil before or after the service. During the service you do and say the right things. You live for God a few hours of the week and then live for yourself the rest of the week.

Women may have problems with pretending to prove that they are right in the sight of God and man. Their voices will be high-pitched, piercing and falsetto, or they will be harsh, rough and angry, or they will be pious, religious and in another tone. In other words their voices will not be natural as if another personality took over and the true personality was submerged.

Men may exhibit their pretense in their overdressing, hair styles, makeup, perfume and jewelry. They pray in a falsetto voice. They try to appear to be very dignified and in control of the situation. They may exhibit false tears for appearance.

Deceit And Deception
It is sad to see the deceit and deception going on in the Christian world today. Most of it stems from those who are trying to build their ministry rather building the Kingdom of God. It is usually self-centered.

Falseness
Anything that is false is contrary to God and will cause us problems of some sort. Falseness can be found in individuals, families, religions, ministries and churches. The human being is trying to be someone other than his natural self.

Cheating
Lying leads to cheating and cheating leads to lying; they work hand-in-hand. Cheating can take on many forms: marriage and family, ministry and church finances, Lord in tithes and offerings, business and income taxes, and in general taking ungodly advantage of others. Cheating on God is called spiritual adultery and whoring after other Gods.

Dishonesty
A dishonest person must lie to cover their tracks. One lie leads to another and the person becomes a compulsive liar. A dishonest Christian will lie to God or try to reason with God about his actions or try to rationalize his actions in his mind. A Christian must first be honest with God and then with themselves. **It is much easier to face the truth headon; in the short run it hurts but in the long run it feels good.**

Responsibility Of A Minister
The minister has a frightening responsibility before God to tell the truth. God holds the teacher to a higher standard than He does the layman that does not teach. The teacher will have to answer to God for every word that he has used to teach God's people. The only relief from that responsibility is that we are constantly learning and will never know it all until God finishes His Training in eternity.

Prayer
Father, I want to be like you; you do not lie. I want the Truth of Jesus Christ to be in me. I repent for being a liar, a deceitful person, being a cheat and dishonest, flattering other

people, giving a false appearance, having pride, ego and vanity, being false and faithless, pretending I am something other than what I am, and for falseness of dress, thoughts and actions. Help me to be what you made me to be; I want to be natural and not false. These things we ask in the Blessed Name of Jesus Christ: Lord, Master and Savior. Amen.

List Of Demons

See the **MASS DELIVERANCE MANUAL** for Lists of Demons that contain word curses such as the following:
Ahab and Jezebel
Charismatic Witchcraft
Common Demon Groupings
Hate, Vengeance, Envy and Strife
Self
Holidays
When Demonization of Christians is Denied

Christian Fantasy - Lies Not Truth

Christian Fantasy and Fables, Christian Tradition and Cliches, Lies, Lying, Deceit, Deception, Ignorance, Laziness, Slothfulness, Playing Church, Play Acting, Lying Teachers and Prophets, False Witness, Falsehood, Pat Phrases, Soulish Prophecy, Spiritual Adultery, False Dreams and Visions, Charismatic Witches and Warlocks, False Prophetesses, Hypocrisy, Vile Affections, Theatrics, Sophistication, Pretension, Divination, False Gifts and Fruits, Greed, Gluttony, Drunkenness, Mind Control, Witchcraft and Rebellion.

Lies, Deceit And Flattery

Lies, Lying, Prevarication, Equivocation, Paltering, Fibbing, Deceitfulness, Deceptiveness, Trickery, Misleading, Deluding, Beguiling, Dishonesty, Unfairness, Mendacious, Untruthful, Flattery, Feigning, Pride, Ego, Vanity, Falseness, Imprudent, Unwise, Faithless, Cheating, Pretending, Insecurity, Inferiority, Rejection, Bitterness, Rebellion, Selfishness, Greediness, Self-Serving, False Witnesses, False Teachers, False Prophets, Fruit of Their Lies, Self-Centered, Spiritual Adultery, Love of Money, Lust of the Eyes, Lust of the Flesh, Pride of Life, Compulsive Liar, Christian Fantasy, Affectation, Theatrics, Playacting, Sophistication, Pretension and Self-Inflated.

Bad Habits Of Thinking And Reacting

Fear of Rejection, Dread, Shame, Fear of Men's Opinions, Apprehension, Sexual Impurity, Fear of Disapproval, Roving, Cult Involvement, Bitterness, Restlessness, Embarrassment, Rebellion, Unreality, Self-Will, Stubbornness, Indifference, Disgust, Anti-Submissiveness, Passivity of Mind, Worry, Disobedience, Lethargy, Anxiety, Fear of Criticism, Depression, Fear of Reproof, Insecurity, Discouragement, Fear of Confrontation, Timidity, Defeatism, Confusion, Inadequacy, Hopelessness, Doubt, Ineptness, Heaviness, Unbelief, Distrust, Burden, Indecision, Fantasy, Forgetfulness, Procrastination, Compromise, Rationalization, Pride, Fear of Failure, Deception, Play-Acting, Ego, Discontent, Frustration, Pretense, Fatigue, Hyperactivity, Argument,

Selfishness, Carelessness, Mockery, Hypocrisy, Heedlessness, Cynicism, Smug Complacency.

SECTION 5 - CURSING OTHERS AND BEING CURSED
(Written By Earline Moody)

CONTENTS
1. COMMENTS
2. SOME THOUGHTS
3. BLESSING OTHERS AND BEING BLESSED
4. PSYCHIC PRAYERS
5. SPOKEN CURSES
6. ANCESTRAL CURSES
7. PARENTAL CURSES
8. CURSING BY OTHERS THAN YOUR ANCESTORS
9. CURSING YOURSELF
10. CURSING YOUR DESCENDENTS
11. ORIGIN OF CURSES
12. BIBLICAL CURSES
13. THE CURSE OF DISOBEDIENCE
14. THE CURSE OF AHAB AND JEZEBEL (BOOKLETS)
15. THE CURSE OF CHARISMATIC WITCHCRAFT
16. THE CURSE OF THE BASTARD (BOOKLET)
17. THE INDIAN CURSES
18. CURSED OBJECTS
19. SUMMARY
20. SPIRITUAL WARFARE
21. LIST OF DEMONS

COMMENTS
This lesson is an overview of curses. See what you think about the following thoughts.

SOME THOUGHTS
It is amazing to me how many areas of the Bible are not explored and taught or preached by the five-fold ministry. It seems like God shows us a never ending list of topics to teach and minister on that are not commonly or frequently taught. Apparently most ministers choose areas of the Bible that they are comfortable with and will further their ministry. The areas that they are not comfortable with, or are controversial, or unpopular, or might cause them to lose some of their congregation or offerings, they avoid like the plague. This may be an excuse before man but it is not an excuse before God, and they will have to answer to Him in the Great Day of Judgement. **Ministers and Christian Leaders - please think about standing before God and explaining why you did not teach certain areas of the Bible.**

Another weakness is the minister that says that you have to keep it simple so that the baby Christians will understand. So, they teach the same thing over and over again. The baby Christians are continually fed milk and are never fed the meat of the Word of God. These Christians never grow up to be mature, strong Christians. Many of these baby

Christians will fall away from Jesus Christ and go back out into the world. **Can you see that the minister is doing his congregation a disservice?**

It is clear that the Body of Christ needs the five-fold ministry which consists of apostles, prophets, evangelists, pastors and teachers. Many pastors would like to make it a four-fold ministry and eliminate the teachers. They say that the pastor is the pastor-teacher and there is no separate teaching ministry. If this is true, then why don't they teach the whole Word of God and not just a part of it? We need teachers who expound the whole Bible in a systematic manner so that the Body of Christ can have a working knowledge of the Bible and put it into practice.

There is a clear difference between preaching and teaching. Preaching is for the moment to stir people up and get them to make decisions in their lives. They walk out of church and usually quickly forget the message. Teaching is for the future to get people to remember the message and apply it to their lives. Teaching gives them a sound foundation to build on and then gives them the structure to build on the foundation.

There are many weaknesses in the church today which cause the Body of Christ to be in a weakened condition. We can not live on emotionalism for long. It makes you feel good for the service but it won't last when the trials of living in this world come to us. We need to have the solid foundation of the Bible to support us in trials and tribulations. It is nice to feel emotional about our salvation. We are not saved by feelings but by our belief in the Word of God.

Another weakness is catering to our fleshly desires. For example, the desire to have possessions. I Tim. 6:10 **For the love of money is the root of all evil: which while some coveted after, they have erred from the faith, and pierced themselves through with many sorrows.** This is teaching the congregation to look to God for blessings and possessions rather than what they can do for God. In other words, praying the give me and mine, my family of four and no more, selfish type of prayer. **Do you agree or disagree with these thoughts?**

BLESSING OTHERS AND BEING BLESSED

There is a lot in the Bible that deals with how to bless others and how to be blessed. This is the balance to cursing others and being cursed. We hear a lot taught about God blessing you but not much taught about how you can bless others in thought, word and deed. The emphasis is on what God will do for you without you having to do anything. Christianity is not a free lunch and we are not on welfare. **To be an effective Christian requires considerable effort.**

There are no blessings in the Bible that are unconditional. For every blessing there is a condition that you must fulfill before you receive the blessing. In other words, this is the **if** you see so often in the verses either stated directly or understood. Deut. 28:1-2 **And it shall come to pass, if thou shalt** (shalt not) **hearken diligently unto the voice of the Lord thy God, to observe and to do all his commandments which I command thee this day, that the Lord thy God will set** (not set) **thee on high above all nations of the**

earth: and all these blessings shall (shall not) **come on thee, and overtake thee, if thou shalt** (shalt not) **hearken unto the voice of the Lord thy God.** The reverse is true also: And it shall come to pass, if thou (shalt not) hearken diligently unto the voice of the Lord thy God, to observe and to do all his commandments which I command thee this day, that the Lord thy God will (not set) thee on high above all nations of the earth: and all these blessings (shall not) come on thee, and overtake thee, if thou (shalt not) hearken unto the voice of the Lord thy God.

PSYCHIC PRAYERS

A psychic prayer is any prayer that does not line up with the Word of God. If you pray contrary to the Bible, then you are praying not to God but to Satan. Satan then has the right before God to loose demons on the people that you prayed for as well as yourself. Praying psychic prayers is a good way to curse others and to be cursed in return.

SPOKEN CURSES

There are two ways that we can curse another person: thought or speaking. We can pray a psychic prayer or we can speak against another person either in our thoughts or out loud. We need to be careful what we think and speak, as well as what we do.

The words we think or speak go out into the air and they have power to do good or evil. Ecc. 10:20 **Curse not the king, no not in thy thought; and curse not the rich in thy bedchamber: for a bird of the air shall carry the voice, and that which hath wings shall tell the matter.** Could this be a demon spirit that God is talking about carrying your thoughts or words to the one that you are thinking or talking about?

ANCESTRAL CURSES

The first curses that we can receive are those placed on us by our ancestors which include our parents. These curses come down the ancestral line and are transferred by familiar spirits that are familiar with our family ancestral sins.

The ancestral curses are started by our ancestors committing some sin against God that is mentioned in the Bible. God would not curse us without warning us beforehand. A good example is the curse of worshiping other Gods. Deut. 5:7-9 **Thou shalt have none other Gods before me. Thou shalt not make thee any graven image, or any likeness of any thing that is in heaven above, or that is in the earth beneath, or that is in the waters beneath the earth: Thou shalt not bow down thyself unto them, nor serve them: for I the Lord thy God am a jealous God, visiting the iniquity of the fathers upon the children unto the third and fourth generation of them that hate me.** If our ancestors worshipped other Gods in the manner described in these verses, then they cursed their descendents to the third and fourth generation. We are innocent and committed no sin but we still are cursed because of what those did who were in authority over us. However, it is not hopeless, God gave us a way to break the curses on us and our descendents.

PARENTAL CURSES

The parents can curse the child in the womb, after the child is born and until it dies. **This is frightening when you think about the consequences of your actions on your children.**

Common examples of cursing the child in the womb include conceiving the child in lust, not wanting the child when it is conceived, and failing in an abortion attempt.

Common examples of cursing the child after it is born include rejecting the child in some manner such as wanting a boy when a girl is born and not quickly changing their minds, cursing the child in thought or words, mistreating the child mentally, physically, spiritually or materially such as physical, emotional and sexual abuse.

CURSING BY OTHERS OTHER THAN YOUR ANCESTORS

You can be cursed by others other than your ancestors. These include those in the grip of the Devil: Satan worshipers, witches and warlocks, covens, fortune tellers and anyone practicing witchcraft. They include those in Christianity who would speak against you and pray psychic prayers for you.

How can you be cursed by these people? Prov. 26:2 **As the bird by wandering, as the swallow by flying, so the curse causeless shall not come.** There must be a cause for the curse to land. We have not seen anyone that lives a blameless, sinless, perfect life according to the whole Word of God. All you have to do is to read or listen to the Bible and see if you fulfill its provisions 100%. **It is very sobering to see how far you miss the target that God set for us to aim at.** We will never be perfect until Jesus Christ finishes the task in the hereafter.

CURSING YOURSELF

Other than being cursed by others, you can curse yourself. You can do this by sinning against God. For example, say that you conceived a bastard before marriage. It does not matter that you then get married; the damage has already been done. Deut. 23:2 **A bastard shall not enter into the congregation of the Lord; even to his tenth generation shall he not enter into the congregation of the Lord.** What you and your girl friend did was to sin by committing fornication, a sin listed in the Bible. Both of you cursed yourselves and ten generations of your descendents with the curse of the bastard. These familiar spirits will work to cause family and church alienation, and a perpetuation of bastards generation after generation.

You can sin against your own body. I Cor. 6:18 **Flee fornication. Every sin that a man doeth is without the body; but he that committeth fornication sinneth against his own body.** This is the only sin that you do that sins against your body and brings curses directly against you. This sin can lead to Hell (spiritual death), physical diseases (physical death or living torment), and many problems in your life (death of marriage, etc.).

CURSING YOUR DESCENDENTS
When you curse yourself, you also curse your descendents. I know of no one-generation curse; they are multiple-generation curses. We have discussed the curse of the bastard and the curse of worshiping other Gods; these carry a ten, and a three to four generation curse respectively.

ORIGIN OF CURSES
Where do curses come from? They come from God and are carried out by Satan with permission from God. Curses can be found listed in the Bible. Satan can not fabricate curses to place on you the way he fabricates lies. Deut. 28:15 **But it shall come to pass, if thou wilt not hearken unto the voice of the Lord thy God, to observe to do all his commandments and his statutes which I command thee this day; that all these curses shall come upon thee, and overtake thee.**

Let's look at where curses come from and where they go: remember that all curses originate with God. **Curses can come to you from your ancestors or those who are not your ancestors, especially those who have authority over you. You can curse yourself. Curses can go out from you to your descendents or to others not your descendents.**

BIBLICAL CURSES
There are probably sixty-six curses that can be easily identified in the Bible by simply looking up the word curse as well as the words cursed and cursing. Most of the curses are not so easily identified but must be discovered by studying the Bible and practicing deliverance. We believe that there is a curse associated with every verse in the Bible that you disobey. Deuteronomy 28 is a chapter of the blessings for obedience and the curses for disobedience. Compare Deut. 28:1-2 (blessings) with 28:15 (curses). Notice the little word **all** and the five times it is used. The corollary to the analogy of all blessings or all curses is that in between all and none are some blessings and some curses. You can be all blessed or all cursed or partially blessed and partially cursed.

THE CURSE OF DISOBEDIENCE
God sends demons and evil on people for disobedience of His Commandments. The following are paraphrases of verses about this subject. He will put a yoke of iron on your neck. Sickness can be caused by demons. God sends evil spirits to do some of His missions. God allowed Satan to prove Job. The deceived and the deceiver are His. He created evil and the waster to destroy. He has deceived and sent strong delusions. He sent a messenger in the flesh. Isa. 45:7 **I form the light, and create darkness: I make peace, and create evil: I the Lord do all these things.**

These actions by God cause many things to happen to people: sickness, cruelty, lying, seduction, death, deceit, troubling, confusion, lethargy, misery, destruction, ignorance, sorrow, wickedness, badness, adversity, affliction, calamity, displeasure, distress, grief, harm, hurt, mischief, sadness, trouble, vex, wretchedness, wrong, perishing, decay, ruin, corruptness, destroying, falling, deluded, allured, enticed, persuaded, slumber, stupor, hardening, deceit, error, etc.

THE CURSE OF AHAB AND JEZEBEL (BOOKLETS)

We have seen the teaching, ministry and counseling about Ahab men and Jezebel women help many people. You can trace these curses back to Adam and Eve in the Garden when they fell from the Grace of God into sin.

Queen Jezebel was a prime example of controlling others. A Jezebelic wife and mother is actually practicing witchcraft as she tries to control her family. Charismatic witches use personal prophecy to control others. Charismatic witches are Jezebels.

THE CURSE OF CHARISMATIC WITCHCRAFT

Another aspect of Ahab and Jezebel is Charismatic Witchcraft. Witchcraft is the practice of trying to control others for personal gain. Charismatic witchcraft is exercising control over other Christians by leaders or by anyone within the congregation. A lot can be written about this subject. There are many demons associated with control of others. This practice is basically mind control.

Soul ties are formed with those to whom we submit our wills. Soul ties can be formed with leaders of the church as well as with anyone in the occult that we go to for help. A dictatorial pastor will form soul ties with his congregation.
The church leaders are cursed by trying to take the place of God in our lives. The congregation is cursed for following man rather than God.

We have no right to control others! God gave us a free will and even He will not try to control us! Therefore, we enter into agreement with Satan and his demons when we attempt to control others, and we are practicing witchcraft!

THE CURSE OF THE BASTARD (BOOKLET)

We believe that probably everyone has the curse of the bastard and the curse of incest on them if they have not forgiven their ancestors, and broken the curse off of them and their descendents. You can see the pattern repeating generation after generation.

THE INDIAN CURSES

Indian curses come from the Indians worshiping idols in their worship services and Indian rites practiced by the tribes. These curses come from worshiping other Gods and practicing the occult.

Earline had Cherokee Indian ancestors on both sides of her family within three generations. Because of these curses, her family had heart trouble and many men died therefrom. Earline, as a woman, even had heart trouble.

The following is her testimony: **I had a heart condition which was unusual. It never occurred with regularity nor under any specific condition. While taking a tread mill test, I experienced tremendous pain in the chest, arms and neck. Having been examined by a 'heart specialist' in Minneapolis, who told me that my heart was good** but he had written 'death by heart attack' on many people's certificates like myself. These were people who didn't really have anything wrong with their hearts.

A year or so after my dad's death I found my heart acting up again. Sometimes one to five years would elapse between seizures. I began to ask God to show me why my brothers, dad, dad's brothers and his dad all had heart problems.

He showed me Exodus 20 and Ezekiel 18. He told me to repent for my ancestors and myself for the sin of idol worship in Leviticus 26:40-41. The curse of idol worship follows the blood line. I did these things and have been free since then. I was only the second generation from previous generations that sinned before God.

Ex. 20:1-6, These are the ten commandments which show the generational curse. Lev. 26:36-42, God promises to remember those that repent. Eze. 18:14-18, We can recover from the sin of our ancestor. **Notice that God will show mercy when we repent.**

CURSED OBJECTS

Deut. 7:26 **Neither shalt thou bring an abomination into thine house lest thou be a cursed thing like it; but thou shalt utterly abhor it for it is a cursed thing.** If you have cursed objects on your body or in your possessions that your carry around, or that are in your home, then your are cursed by God. You have invited the demons to attack you and the people that live in your home.

My favorite example is pierced ears which is a sign of slavery in the Bible. Jesus Christ wants us to live a simple life without religious objects or graven images. If the men take off religious objects and the women to take off jewelry except for wedding rings and watches, this will help in the deliverance to get rid of the demons.

SUMMARY

Therefore, be very careful how you think, pray, speak and act. Study your Bible to find out how God thinks and acts so that you can think, speak, pray and act in accordance with His Will. Also study to see how you should bless, rather than curse, others as well as yourself and your family.

Obey and be blessed - disobey and be cursed! It's your choice. You will be blessed in proportion to the amount of the Bible you follow and cursed in proportion to the amount of the Bible you do not follow. **We are told to keep all the words of the Holy Bible.**

SPIRITUAL WARFARE

Periodically, Earline and I had to break the curses that are placed against us and our ministry. You can feel the spiritual pressure building up and it is necessary to go to spiritual war. We forgive those who knowingly or unknowingly are praying or speaking against us, break any curses or soul ties, send the demons back to those who sent them, and pray that their eyes will be opened.

PRAYER - Father, we want to bless others and be blessed rather than to curse others and be cursed. Please make us a blessing and take away the curse. We will get rid of cursed objects in our possession. We ask that you, other people and our descendents forgive us for anything we have done to bring the curse. We forgive our ancestors and everyone else that have placed curses on us. Please forgive these people for psychic prayers, spoken curses, ancestral curses, parental curses, cursing by others, cursing ourselves, cursing our descendents, disobedience, Ahab and Jezebel, charismatic witchcraft, conceiving bastards, having incest, Indian curses, and any other curse known or unknown that is found in the Holy Word of God.

I now break any curses placed on me or my descendents from uttering a wish of evil against one; to imprecate evil, to call for mischief or injury to fall upon; to execrate, to bring evil upon or to; to blast, vex, harass or torment with great calamities. I break the curses back to ten generations or even to Adam and Eve on both sides of my family, and destroy every legal hold and every legal ground that demons have to work in my life. I break curses that follow in the name of the Lord Jesus Christ.

- Mistreating God's Chosen People
- Adultery, Harlotry, Prostitution
- Idolatry
- Refusing To Fight For God
- Not Giving To Poor
- Swearing Falsely By God
- Robbing God of Tithes
- Hearkening to Wives Rather Than God
- Cheating People Out of Property
- Oppressing Strangers, Widows, Orphans
- Incest With Sister or Mother
- Pride
- Doing The Work of God Deceitfully
- Abortion or Causing Unborn To Die
- Murdering Indirectly
- Kidnapping
- Not Preventing Death
- Witchcraft
- Following Horoscopes
- Losing Virginity Before Marriage
- Rape
- Teaching Rebellion Against God
- Refusing To Warn Sinners
- Sacrificing Humans
- Intercourse During Menstruation
- Necromancers
- Being Carnally Minded
- Children Rebelling
- Fugitive and Vagabond
- Willing Deceivers
- Disobedience to Bible
- Keeping Cursed Objects
- House of Wicked
- Stealing
- Failing To Give Glory to God
- Dishonoring Parents
- Making Graven Images
- Taking Advantage of Blind
- Bestiality
- Murder Secretly or For Hire
- Putting Trust In Man
- Rewarding Evil For Good
- Having Bastards
- Striking Parents
- Cursing Parents
- Sacrificing to Gods
- Turning Someone Away From God
- Rebelling Against Pastors
- False Prophets
- Not Disciplining Children
- Cursing Rulers
- Defiling The Sabbath
- Seances and Fortune Telling
- Homosexuals and Lesbians
- Blaspheming Lord's Name
- Oral and Anal Sex
- Nonproductivity
- Improper Family Structure

Destruction of Family Priesthood
Family Disorder
Any Sin Worthy of Death
Any Biblical Curse Not listed
Choosing That Which God Delights Not In
Offending Children Believing Christ
Adding To or Taking Away From Bible
Refusing To Do The Word of God
Failure and Poverty
Touching God's Anointed
Above Perversion of Gospel
Looking To World For Help
Stubbornness and Rebellion
Loving Cursing

LIST OF DEMONS
Call out the demons that come in through the curses also.

Pestilence
Consumption
Fever
Inflammation
Extreme Burning
Blasting
Mildew
Botch of Egypt
Emerods
Scab
Itch
Madness
Blindness
Astonishment of Heart
Plagues
Sore Sicknesses
Diseases of Egypt
Trembling of Heart
Failing of Eyes
Sorrow of Mind
Broken Vows
Unicorn
Twelve Petal Rosette
Love & Romance
Pentacle/Pentagram
Star of David
White Magic
Italian Horn
Egyptian Ankh
Mexican Sun God

Idol Worship
Bastard
Wicked Balances
Dislike/Hatred/Murder
Curse of the Law
Bless You Spirits
Incest
Lesbians
Necromancers
Blaspheming
Sodomy
Oral & Anal Sex
Slackness
Deeper Teachings
Irish Shamrock Hex
Fertility
Deceiving
Adultery
Disobedience
Cursed Objects
Thievery
False Swearing
The Distlefink
Eight Pointed Star
Eastern Star
Mogen David
Masonic Symbols
Leprechaun's Staff
Egyptian Sun God RA
Buddhas

Graven Images
Pride
Catholic Prayers
Prince of Southern Curses
Prince of Occult
Witchcraft Curses
Voodoo Curses
Occult Curses
American Indian Curses
Charismatic Witchcraft
Horoscopes
Rebellion
False Prophets
Seances
Fortune Telling
Nonproductivity
Personal Poverty
Misrepresentation
Perversion of Judgment
Doubt
Homosexual
Tulip
Your Lucky Stars
Friendship Hex
Hexagram
Cabalistic Magic Symbol
Freemasonry
Unicorn's Horn
Zodiac
Crescent Moon & Star

Cursing, Vexation, Rebuke, Destroying, Perishing, Consuming, Groping
Not Prosper, Oppressed, Spoiled, Failure, Crushed, Smite, Pursuing
Sore Botch of Knees, Legs and Whole Body
Overtaking, Distress, Plucked, Chastisement, Removed, Not Healed

Astonishment, Proverb, Byword, Want, Besiege, Straitness, Evil

Emotionalism, Love of Money, Psychic Prayers, Idol Worship, Conceived in Lust, Abortion, Rejection, Physical Abuse, Emotional Abuse, Sexual Abuse, Bastard, Incest, Fornication, Strife, Alienation, Sickness, Deceit, Delusions, Cruelty, Lying, Seduction, Death, Troubling, Confusion, Lethargy, Misery, Destruction, Ignorance, Sorrow, Wickedness, Badness, Adversity, Affliction, Calamity, Displeasure, Distress, Grief, Harm, Hurt, Mischief, Sadness, Trouble, Vex, Wretchedness, Wrong, Perishing, Decay, Ruin, Corruptness, Destroying, Falling, Deluded, Allured, Enticed, Persuaded, Slumber, Stupor, Hardening, Error, Taking God's Glory, Following Man, Witchcraft, Indian Spirits

SECTION 6 - HOUSE CURSES
Written By Earline Moody

CONTENTS
1. SCRIPTURES
2. TESTIMONIES
    1. Seven-month Old Child
    2. Marie Moody
    3. Asian People
3. SHOULD HOUSES BE CLEANSED OF EVIL SPIRITS?
4. CURSED OBJECTS AND POSSESSIONS
    1. Cursed Objects
    2. A Word About Incense
    3. Cursed Objects and Demon Infestation
    4. Cursed and Inanimate Objects
    5. Summary
5. SIGNS AND SYMBOLS
    1. Hex Signs
    2. Symbols of Hex Signs
    3. Masonic Symbols
    4. Symbols
6. TOYS
    1. Dolls
    2. Dolls in Toledo, Ohio
    3. Baby - Seven Months Old
    4. Satan In The Toy Store
    5. Toys Having Either Occult Linkage,
    6. Actions or Excessive Violence
    7. Summary of Toys
7. CLEANING YOUR HOUSE OF DEMONIC OBJECTS
    1. To Exorcise Inanimate Objects
    2. Five Steps To Cleaning House
8. PRAYER
9. REFERENCES

SCRIPTURES
"L" is scripture for lesson; "C" is scripture for cleaning your house:

L - Ex. 20:4 Graven Image (Jesus' picture? He did not have white skin!)
C - Num. 23:8 & 23 Can only curse if God curses (notice that God curses).
L -   Deut. 7:25-26 Those who keep or own cursed objects (you are cursed).
L - Deut. 14:7-19 Unclean animals (something for you to think about).
C - Deut. 21:23 Anyone hanged is accursed of God.
C - Deut. 32:5,17 Have corrupted themselves. Have worshipped devils (demons).
C - Josh. 6:18 Those who keep or own cursed objects (are cursed).

C - II Sam. 7:29 Blessing of the Lord.
L - Prov. 3:33 Curse of the Lord on house of the wicked.
L - Jer. 48:10 Deceitful worker of the Lord is cursed.
C - Gal. 3:13 Christ has redeemed us from the curse (must be applied).
C - Col. 2:14-15 Blotting out ordinances against us.
L - II Tim. 4:4 They will not endure sound doctrine.
C - Rev. 12:11 Overcome by word of testimony.
C - Rev. 22:3 No more curse in Heaven.

TESTIMONIES
Seven-Month Old Child

Earline and I were working with a mother and her child who was seven-months old. As we were taking the mother through prayers for her sins, the child spoke and said, **NO GENE NO**. As you know, children of this age can not speak. What do you think spoke through the child - a demon?

Marie Moody

Some friends of ours were ministers who went to Haiti. One time they brought us some carved figurines as a gift. These statutes caused us strife in the family. Our daughter, Marie, felt like there were eyes watching her as she walked across the room. The Lord finally got our attention and we destroyed the wood figures. The wood would not burn normally and finally I had to soak them in charcoal-lighter fluid. When they finally burned, a green flame came out and shot toward us. These dolls were probably made by Voodoo worshipers who blessed them so that they would be sold. After getting rid of the statutes, the strife left our family. What do you think the green flame was - a demon?

Asian People

One of my favorite examples is that of the Buddha. Do you have a cute little Buddha sitting in your house? If so, you are cursed because you have a cursed object in your home.

Another example is the family alter for worship of dead ancestors. This is spiritual idolatry and brings curses to the family.

God took Pastor Jesse Duplantis to Heaven while he was alive. He saw many Asian children but few Asian adults. Apparently the Asian world is caught in a death trap of Asian religions and will go to Hell. Asia has half of the world population. The children are innocent if they die before the age of accountability and will go to Heaven.

An Asian church was meeting in an Odd Fellow Lodge. This is Masonry, a false religion, and cursed the church. Who knows how much damage was done?

SHOULD HOUSES BE CLEANSED OF EVIL SPIRITS? (EXCERPTS)

Due to my involvement with demons through deliverance, I have heard many reports of unusual demon activities in connection with houses and objects. **Books and objects identified with anything related to Satan's kingdom have been known to attract** demons. **Sinful activities on the part of former residents account for some houses needing to be cleansed.**

Many have told of hearing voices or sounds in their houses. Such manifestations are sometimes called **poltergeist**, a German word meaning **knocking or noisy ghosts**.

What about the owls and frogs? These are classified among the creatures mentioned in Deut. 14:7-19 as being unclean and abominable. They are types of demon spirits.

The graven images of their Gods you shall burn with fire, you shall not desire the silver or gold that is on them, nor take it for yourself, lest you be ensnared by it; for it is an abomination to the Lord your God. Neither shall you bring an abomination (an idol) into your house, lest you be ensnared by it; for it is an abomination to the Lord your God (Deut. 7:25-26).

Demons are definitely attracted to houses by objects and literature that pertain to false religions, cults, the occult and spiritism. All such materials should be burned or otherwise destroyed. Houses or buildings which are suspect of demon infestation should be cleansed by the authority of the name of Jesus. Those who live in such places should stand on the provisions of the blood of Jesus Christ. **(Probably the greatest abomination to God is worshiping other Gods in any form such as having an idol in your house.)**

NOTES ON WITCHCRAFT, SYMBOLS AND ACCURSED OBJECTS
(EXCERPTS)

In Satan worship, often times the arms are crossed as a sign of submission to and being bound by the devil. **(Also a sign of rebellion.)**

Often good luck charms, ankhs, astrological symbols and other jewelry with hex signs, etc. will cause interference with deliverance. Some objects, particularly rings, bracelets, necklaces and other jewelry which has been given to a person by someone in witchcraft, will have curses and bring bondage with them.

There is a resurgence of hex signs, and ancient geometric and mystical motifs which are being incorporated into designs for clothing, jewelry, decorative objects and china. In antique shops there are often selections of rings, pendants, pins and various kinds of jewelry which were originally designed to bring good luck and to act as a talisman to chase evil. Some of the most popular currently include: The Egyptian ankh (a cross with a loop at the top which was an ancient fertility symbol); the ancient witchcraft sign of the broken cross, popularly known as the peace symbol; Chais (consists of Hebrew characters spelling the word life); Polynesian tikkis, figures and other things; a wiggly tail which is called the **Italian horn**; protectors from the evil eye; a hand with the index and little fingers pointing up (a satanic witchcraft sign); and a great variety of crosses, clovers, stars, wishbones, lucky coins, mystic medals, horseshoes and other items.

Another interesting thing is how many times in religious fetishes and statues there is a dangerous resident demon power.

If it is necessary to do deliverance in a house, it is wise to clean the house spiritually afterward, to head off any trouble which might be caused by spirits remaining in the place. **(Command the demons to leave the people, house and property.)**

CURSED OBJECTS AND POSSESSIONS
Cursed Objects (Excerpts)

Believers who have broken with Freemasonry and renounced their vows, should write to the lodge asking that their names be **deleted from the membership roll**. It is also important that personal regalia (or those handed down in the family) should be destroyed. Associated clothing should be burnt, and metal objects including swords defaced, or smashed and disposed of. Relatives are sometimes superstitious about disposing of these **family relics**, but they are cursed, and if retained will bring the judgment of God upon the household.

Demons may try to prevent Masonic objects from being destroyed by hiding the means of destruction or preventing the objects from being destroyed such as preventing the objects from catching on fire.

A Word About Incense (Excerpts)

Believers must be careful about bringing incense into their homes. Most people are unaware that much of the incense sold in curio and novelty shops was manufactured by devotees of the Hare Krishna cult. Their wares are dedicated to this demon God of the Hindus and can cause much trouble.

Cursed Objects And Demon Infestation (Excerpts)

This is just a partial list of many objects that attract demons. It is recommended that two Christians, in agreement, led by The Holy Spirit, go through the dwelling to discern demonic objects that need to be destroyed. It is up to the owner what will be destroyed. A recommended book is **Masonic And Occult Symbols Illustrated** by Cathy Burns, Sharing, Mt. Carmel, PA.

Crosses, pictures and objects may be Godly or ungodly. For instance, there are ungodly crosses. Ex. 20:4 **Thou shalt not make unto thee any graven image, or any likeness of any thing that is in heaven above, or that is in the earth beneath, or that is in the water under the earth.** This is a key verse to use in discernment.

Cast demons out of houses; command demons to go by these names or associated with these objects:
1. Books and objects identified with anything related to Satan's Kingdom.
2. Sinful activities of former residents left **curses**.
3. Knocking or noisy ghosts (poltergeist) and apparitions.
4. Owl and frog images.
5. Witch's mask and fetishes used by witch doctors.

6. Objects and literature that pertain to false religions, cults, the occult and spiritism.
7. Graven images of Gods (demons).
8. Objects dedicated to demons (idols and artifacts).
9. Ouija boards or other occult paraphernalia.
10. Prayers and worship to demons bring **curses** on home.
11. Mexican sun Gods; idols, incense; Buddhas; hand carved objects from Africa or the Orient; anything connected with astrology, horoscopes, fortune telling, etc.; books or objects associated with witchcraft, good luck charms or cult religions (metaphysics, Christian Science, Jehovah's Witnesses, etc.); rock and roll records and tapes.
12. Jewelry given to a person by someone in witchcraft, hex signs, ancient geometric and mystical motifs. Jewelry designed to bring good luck and act as talisman to chase evil.
13. Egyptian ankh, broken cross (peace symbol), chais, Polynesian tikkis of Gods, African jujus, Italian horn, protectors from the evil eye, hand with index and little fingers pointing up, clovers, stars, wishbones, lucky coins, mystic medals, horseshoes, religious fetishes and statues.
14. Products with cryptic curses **(hidden, secret, occult curses)**.
15. Dolls used for witchcraft and magic; puppets, cult objects or representations.
16. **Common familiars** include occult objects used in practice of occult arts; Rock & Roll records, tapes, posters and T-shirts; occultic role-playing fantasy games; artifacts of Eastern religions such as statues of Gods; rosaries, crucifixes and pictures of statues of Catholic saints; objects used in the practice of Catholicism and Masonry; literature and tapes on the occult and pagan religions; New Age and Rock & Roll subliminal-suggestion tapes; and similar items. **There is no way to come up with a complete list.**

Cursed And Inanimate Objects

If you have a cursed object, you become cursed by God! Remove cursed objects from your being and from your home; destroy by breaking, burning or at least throw them in the trash can. Do not keep the cursed silver or gold of the object. If the cursed object belongs to someone else and you can not throw it away, then anoint with oil and cast the demons out of it. Anoint your house with oil and cast out evil spirits from your house and possessions.

You must clean your home and your body of cursed objects. If you have cursed objects, you become cursed and you will have demons living with you. They don't just come to live in your home or on your person, they come to torment you and your family.

If you have cursed objects on your body or in your possessions that your carry around, or that are in your home, then your are cursed by God. You have invited the demons to attack you and the people that live in your home.

My favorite example is pierced ears which is a sign of slavery in the Bible. Jesus Christ wants us to live a simple life without religious objects or graven images. I want the men to take off religious objects. I want the women to take off jewelry except for wedding rings and watches. This will help in the deliverance to get rid of the demons.

Summary

If you have a cursed object in your house, you are cursed. A cursed object does not just sit idle in your house. It will cause trouble for you. There are demons that live in or around the cursed object. **Do you feel an unusual attraction or repulsion to some object in your home, office or car?** You may have a demonic tie to it.

SIGNS AND SYMBOLS
Hex Signs (Excerpts)

The five pointed star has been used by witches for centuries and called the pentacle or pentagram. With the two points up (as in Eastern Star) it is called the sign of the goat or Satan; one point up symbolizes witchcraft. When witches want to talk with demons, they will often stand within a pentagram and the demon will appear within a six pointed star by two triangles (hexagram) commonly called the Star of David. The Mogen David, as it was called, was a Cabalistic magic symbol for white magic and the word hex comes from the hexagram.

Masonic symbols were ancient witchcraft signs long before freemasonry was created. The initiation rituals for witchcraft and Masons are identical (according to ex-witch John Todd), again demonstrating Masonic roots into witchcraft. The only difference is that the initiated witch disrobes completely at the close, and signs in his own blood.

The wiggly horn called the Italian horn is also a witchcraft device (leprechaun's staff or unicorn's horn) and means you trust the Devil for your finances.

The Egyptian ankh (cross with a loop on top) is a sex Goddess symbol meaning you despise virginity, believe in fertility rites, and worship and serve the Egyptian sun God RA (Egyptian name for Lucifer).

The signs of the Zodiac are occult symbols as are the little Mexican sun Gods and Buddhas. The crescent moon and star are the sign of an initiate into witchcraft.

In the Old Testament, God gave cunning skills to hands of artisans who fashioned the furnishings and decorations for the tabernacle. The use of these signs and symbols, and others which are the property of Satan can bring demons to your home and/or person.

Symbols Of Hex Signs (Excerpts)

Remove these symbols from your person and possessions:
1. Six Petal Rosette and Lucky Stars - these are your lucky stars.
2. The Irish Shamrock Hex - good luck, fast life, good fortune and fidelity.
3. Tulip - faith, hope and charity.
4. Unicorn - virtue and piety.
5. Fertility.
6. Twelve Petal Rosette - that each month of the year be joyous ones.
7. The Distelfink - the bird of happiness always near you and good fortune.
8. Your Lucky Stars - lucky stars that guide your heart.

9. Love and Romance - rosette and hearts of love and romance.
10. Eight Pointed Star - star and rosette to bring abundance and goodwill.
11. Friendship.
12. There is a symbol for each of the above listed hex signs.

Masonic Symbols (Excerpts)

There are many **Masonic trinkets and tokens, and jewels and regalia** which cause trouble for Christians. Symbols are disguised. **Baphomet is the satanic Goat of Mendes** and the best known representation of Lucifer in occultism. **Caduceus** is an emblem of the **Supreme Deity of the Masons** and represented the active power of generation and the passive power of production conjoined. **Inverted pentagram** is to call up the power of Satan and is one of the main symbols of witchcraft and occultism. **Square and compass** symbolize the human reproductive organs, locked in coitus. **Crescent moon and star** are used by witches. **Lambskin apron** is an emblem of innocence and the badge of a Mason. **Hexagram** is a powerful symbol to witches, sorcerers and magicians.

Symbols

1. Many symbols are of demonic origin such as Fleur-de-Lis. Britannica Encyclopedia gives this explanation. In India and in Egypt it was common decorating device used as a symbol of life and resurrection, the attribute of the God Horus.
2. The Mobile Winged horse - Pegasus; FTD's symbol is Mercury or Hermes - the messenger of the Gods, God of commerce also God of fraud and cunning.
3. Caduceus the winged wand of Mercury - Doctors and the American Medical Profession.
4. Nike is the Goddess of victory (Athena).
5. The cornucopia represents the goat mother (Amaltheia) who suckled the infant-God in a cave; Zeus is said to have given it to her to insure a plenteous supply of food.

When you read the scripture given at the beginning of this lesson you probably began to feel that the Gods and Goddess, and mythology is a collection of demon worship. Many of the Gods and Goddess are referred to in the Old Testament by the names the Hebrews would have used. They come from the old Chaldean Religion. Tammuz is mentioned in the Bible. The references to groves, temple prostitution, etc. is about idol worship or demon worship. Everyone should do a little research into this and discover the original reason for our holidays and symbols. Old encyclopedias are better than later editions because the later editions leave out much information that is vital to us. Research the meaning of Biblical references to groves, temples, temple prostitutes, and celebrations in both Old and New Testaments. It will open you eyes to the revival of Satan and demon worship in America, and to our coming judgement. God did not overlook the Hebrews worship of Satan and the demons, and He promises not to overlook ours either.

To really follow God, demands that as soon as you learn of something you do or have that is an abomination to God, you remove it from your life immediately. Your Christian friends may not agree with you and may criticize you. After you have done your research and have submitted it to God, you follow His direction.

TOYS
Dolls (Excerpts)

Dolls were believed to bring good luck to their owners, to make livestock give more milk, help win wars and heal the sick. Only witch doctors or medicine men were allowed to handle them.

The **dictionary** defines a doll as a small carved or molded figure which served as a cult object or representation of a nursery story, cartoon or puppet character.

Both **World Book** and **Britannica** point out that dolls were buried with people and were supposed to be friends and servants in the spirit world.

Roman and Greek girls, in preparation for marriage would leave their dolls on the altar of the temples of Artemis and Diana. **To this day multitudes of idol (demon) worshippers use dolls in pagan religious ceremonies.**

In ancient times the worship of idols included the offering of various types of sacrifices, libations and other acts of devotion such as kissing an image, kneeling or dancing before it. On occasion the worshiper inflicted wounds in themselves as a special act of homage. The second commandment of the Decalogue prohibited the making of any image of The God Of Israel. Despite the fact that arks, ephods and terraphin found their place in the religion of Israel, not a single figure of God has ever been recovered by archaeologists. This feature of Israel's religion sharply distinguished it from that of her neighbors and contemporaries, and profoundly attests to the fact that the true God is not a being whose personality can be adequately reflected in the products of human handicrafts. Idolatry was a constant problem in ancient Israel.

Dolls In Toledo, Ohio (Excerpts)

One night when my wife was complaining to me about the child's insolence, out of nowhere I said, **Her problems are those stinking doll babies, it's witchcraft.**

The next night while I was praying for someone's deliverance, she picked up an **encyclopedia** to check what it said about dolls! There it was: **origin in witchcraft and magic.**

Baby - Seven Months Old (Excerpts)

The Lord began to show us the legal grounds Satan held. It was in his dolls! He had received one for Christmas and a small plastic boy sailor doll at birth. The Lord also told my husband of various stuffed toys (in shapes of animals - whales, dogs and kangaroos), a plastic toy **Big Bird** and matching bib. These were thrown away and curses from them broken. **(Look for strange sicknesses or diseases that will not heal in children.)**

When the Lord commanded that **no graven images** were to be made, He wasn't being cruel and heartless. He knew the damage they could put upon people (Ex. 20:4). The Lord has also shown us that puppets are a deception and the Lord places a curse on those that use deceit (Jer. 48:10).

Satan In The Toy Store

And changed the glory of the incorruptible God into an image made like to corruptible man, and to birds, and four footed beasts, and creeping things (Rom. 1:23).

There shall not be found among you anyone that maketh his son or his daughter to pass through the fire, or that useth divination, or an observer of times, or an enchanter, or a witch, Or a charmer, or a consulter with familiar spirits, or a wizard, or a necromancer. For all that do these things are an abomination unto the LORD: and because of these abominations the LORD thy God doth drive them out from before thee (Deut. 18:10-12). The permissive society along with its blinding perversion of moral and spiritual values is an appalling reality.

How can a child be influenced to readily accept demons? **Webster's defines fantasy as 1) imagination or fancy, especially wild, visionary fancy; 2) unreal mental image; illusion; phantasm; 3) whim; queer notion; caprice; 4) an imaginative poem, play, etc. and 5) in psychology, a mental image as in a day dream.**

Movies - Demonic movies aim to frighten, to deceive, to familiarize children with hideous characters, to entice children to accept evil as good, etc. **Woe to those who call evil good and good evil (Isa.5:20).**

For instance, consider E.T. He could heal, raise the dead, etc.; a mockery of Jesus and a horrible creature. Movies to avoid are Star Wars, Dark Cauldrons, Rosemary's Baby, The Exorcist and similar movies.

Fairy Tales and Walt Disney - Time Warner movies are full of cabalistic practices such as **The Chronicles of Narina: the Lion, the Witch and the Wardrobe** and Time Warner's - Harry Potter Movies - **The Lord of the Rings**. These movies and books help the children to accept the menacing demons as their friends. They no longer have fear if these devils appear to them in their rooms. They become their **imaginary friends**. In actuality, they are malignant evil spirits, sent to rob, kill and destroy the children.

Read Daniel 11:38; God of forces means munitions. The below games include force or munitions. In the games munitions is associated with occult, charms and magic.

Years ago God showed me the reason for Walt Disney movies, full of occult workings and such as E.T. It was to get the children to feel comfortable, even to love the better of the evil presented to them. Do you think it has worked?

In our work with people, we have found fantasy to be a major problem. Many people under 35 years old have a hard time living in a real world. Dwelling in fantasy has become to them the real world; the real world is fantasy. Fantasy costs in lost mental power, satisfaction of life and work.

Cartoons draw on Egyptology - Isis; mythology, witchcraft, occult, Smurfs, Dungeons & Dragons, Little People and Gremlins. The most violent block of T.V. time is Saturday morning aimed to steal the souls of children.

Fairy Tales and Walt Disney movies are full of occult practices: Mary Poppins, Dark Cauldron, etc. Video games incite destruction and death.

Rock music and subliminal music is meant to operate on stimuli that exist below the threshold of the conscious mind. Its goal is to awaken the energy center (in the brain) and to expand mental awareness. Scientific instruments have proved it reaches its goal. Music is more powerful than drugs.

New Age Children's music is to incite rebellion and self elevation. Rock music leads young people into sexual perversions and violence.

Toys Having Either Occult Linkage, Actions Or Excessive Violence
These can cause demonic possession in children. SMURFS: (German word for demon) - Papa Smurf is a wizard who casts spells and mixes potions, and often refers to Beelzebub (Satan) in the cartoons. He practices sorcery and witchcraft.

Wizards and witches were put to death in the Old Testament. Paying heed to them, however amusing or cute and innocent they seem to be, gives respectability to that which God forbids. He knows it leads to one opening up oneself to satanic bondage. Ignore and Renounce!

STAR WARS: The theme is based on a cosmic force taken from Zen Buddhism and Eastern religions. **EMPIRE STRIKES BACK:** Yoda is referred to as a Zen master. **E.T. TOYS:** E.T. levitates, uses mental telepathy, heals supernaturally, resurrected, imitation of the life of Jesus, operates in the occult. **DUNGEON'S AND DRAGONS:** Fantasy game fought in the minds of the players. Teaches demonology, witchcraft, voodoo, murder, rape, blasphemy, suicide, assassination, insanity, sex perversion, homosexuality, Satan worship, barbarianism, cannibalism, sadism, demon summoning, necromancy and divination. Human sacrifice. Some game!!

RAINBOW BRITE AND SPRITES: Sprites are listed in the advanced D & D Monster Manual. New Age Movement uses rainbow symbol with the star. **SHE-RA:** Princess of power, magic power, female defender of the universe. RA is the name of Egyptian sun God. **PEGASUS:** Flying horse from D & D monster manual. New Age Movement uses it for astral flight/meditation. **UNICORNS:** D & D Monster Manual; Medieval kings and popes used amulet made from horn; believed to have magical and healing powers. **CARE BEARS:** (Not Really???) Wear charms (amulets) to keep away evil spirits (occult symbols). Rabbit foot, rainbow with star (New Age symbol) horseshoe, four leaf clover. Latest character, wizard.

HERSELF THE ELF: Elves are inferior spirit beings with great powers supposedly. Magical flowers. **MAGIC KIT:** It's magic, spirit slate with mystery computer. Teaches how to become a magician. **CABBAGE PATCH DOLLS:** Creates soul tie with child; mockery of life and death and natural emotions. **CABBAGE PATCH PLAYMATES** - (to promote illegitimacy) - Amulets Koosas - mysterious cuddly creature which brings good luck - adoptable - you name them. **PUNK ROCK DOLL:** Name and adopt, same as above. **GREMLINS:** Violent, sadistic; use transformation (New Age concept), Cannibalism, and promotional scheme. From English word germane to vex. Kill and viciously attack people.

CROSSBOWS & CATAPULTS: Designed from **Dark Ages**; Vikings vs. Barbarians, very violent. Fantasy. **SWORD & SORCERY BATTLE GEAR:** Fantasy, sorcery, occult, violence. **G.I. JOE:** Now adding occult characters to their ranks of regular army characters. **STARRIORS:** Warrior robots kill for control of earth using chain saws, buzz saw, drills, spiked ream, vibrator chisel. **SECRET WARS:** Fight aliens with secret messages (occult); the 'Force', wild mutants and hideous creature transformation. **OTHER WORLD:** Similar to D & D. Violence with warlords, demons, dragons. **BLACK STAR:** Warlock with alien demon; similar to D & D. **BLACKSTONE:** Teaches magic.

MASTERS OF THE UNIVERSE: Evil Lords of destruction, beast man, evil ocean warlord...sorcery. Trying to take the place of Jesus as protector of His creation. **TRANSFORMER:** New Age concept. The deceptive leader promotes peace through tyranny. Links up to Black Hole. Occult practice can change body into another form. **SNAKE MOUNTAIN:** Player becomes the snake and works the demon's jaws as he speaks. Experiment with demon power. **ROBO FORCE:** Evil Robot Empire, very violent, **He has killer instinct and a crusher hand.** Dictator and destroyer. **GO BOTS:** Alien robots? Transformation into vehicles. Confuse good and evil.

BOARD GAMES: These games open children to the influence of occult power, wizardry, violence, mind control and witchcraft: Thundar-Barbarian, Pandemonium, Magic 8 Ball, Monster Mansion, Krull (occult with sorcerer), Herself the Elf, Gremlins, Dragon Master, Mythical Cards, Dungeon, Ouija, Dark Towers, Magical Crystals, Dragon Lords, Towers of Night, Forest of Doom, Fires of Shadarr, Star Wars and Yoda, Fantasy Card Game, Hell Pits of Night-Fang, Rune Quest, Chivalry, Sorcery and Arduin-Grimoire.

Summary of Toys
II Timothy 4:4 - **In the last days they will not endure sound DOCTRINE. They shall turn away their ears from hearing the truth; they shall turn unto FABLES and MYTHS!** Webster's Dictionary defines FABLES: fictitious narrative, legendary story of supernatural happenings, a narrative story in which animals SPEAK AND ACT LIKE HUMAN BEINGS. Beware Christian, these are the END TIMES!

CLEANING YOUR HOUSE OF DEMONIC OBJECTS
To Exorcise Inanimate Objects (Excerpts)
In the case of objects dedicated to demons (idols, artifacts, etc.), the best course of action is to destroy them. However, it is well to check secondhand cars, homes and

apartments also because if the former owners had ouija boards, or other occult paraphernalia, or were involved in serious bondage to sin, then there is every reason to suspect that evil spirits could be lingering behind. These spirits can and will cause trouble to the new owners.

Keep in mind that any prayers offered to anyone or anything other than God the Father, Son and Holy Spirit constitute prayers and/or worship to demons. Very often these are answered in the form of curses, for demons can and do respond to those who request of them. **(If you know of demonic prayers against your family, break the curses placed against you.)**

We suggest that two believers go on a mission such as this with Bible in hand. These should be destroyed. Look for little Mexican sun Gods, idols, incense, Buddhas, hand carved objects from Africa or the Orient, Ouija boards, anything connected with astrology, horoscopes, fortune telling and so on. Books or objects associated with witchcraft, good luck charms, or the cult religions (metaphysics, Christian Science, Jehovah's Witnesses, etc.), rock and roll records and tapes fall in the category of things which have been often loaded with evil spiritual power.

Verbally denounce Satan and his power, and his demon hosts and claim authority as a believer-priest because of the name of Jesus Christ and the authority of His shed Blood. **(There is more power in the spoken word.)**

Some Scripture which has proven useful in this includes: Rev. 12:11; 22:3; Col. 2:14-15; Gal. 3:13; Deut. 21:23; 32:5 & 17; Num. 23:8, 23; II Sam. 7:29. **(Read out loud in the house.)**

The door lintel and window sills should be anointed by touching them with olive oil. Other things such as statues have been so anointed in Jesus name and many times the demonic power is checked or destroyed. Any specific areas of demonic activity or influence of which you are aware should be denounced by name (Prov. 3:33). **(This should be done for objects that you don't own and can not destroy.)**

Five Steps To Cleaning House
Worshiping other Gods is spiritual adultery:
1. Five-way prayer of forgiveness - **you forgive your ancestors, descendants and others**, ask God to forgive and bless them. **Ask God to forgive you; you forgive yourself for sins against your body**. Also ask forgiveness for spiritual adultery.
2. Break curses and soul ties from others and to others. Break curses of psychic or Catholic prayers.
3. Clean out house of those objects or exorcise objects you don't own.
4. Anoint house with oil and drive evil spirits out of house.
5. Cast demons out of people that came in thru curses from objects.

PRAYER

Lord, I come to you about cursed objects and demon infestation in my possessions and home, and in me. I forgive my ancestors, descendants and others who have had spiritual influence over me. I ask you to forgive and bless them, especially with salvation. Please forgive me and I forgive myself for spiritual adultery. I forgive those who have cursed me; forgive me for cursing others. I break the curses and demonic soul ties including psychic and Catholic prayers. I will clean out my house of cursed objects or exorcise objects that I don't own. I will anoint my house with oil and drive the evil spirits out of the house. Show me cursed objects, demon infestation and spirits that need to be cast out of people. In Jesus Name I pray.

REFERENCES

Battling The Hosts Of Hell; Conquering The Hosts Of Hell; Demolishing The Hosts Of Hell; Annihilating The Hosts Of Hell, Volumes I and II; Eradicating The Hosts Of Hell; Smashing The Hosts Of Hell; The Alcoholic Syndrome; Grappling with the Host of Hell; Freedom from the Hosts of Hell; and **Harassing The Host of Hell**, eleven books (and fifty booklets covering particular topics) by Win Worley, Hegewisch Baptist Church, Highland, Indiana

Pigs In The Parlor by Frank Hammond, Impact Christian Books

SECTION 7 - IDOLATRY CURSES

CONTENTS
1. **EZEKIEL 8:5-18**
   1. King James Version
   2. Amplified Version
2. **IDOLATRY**
3. **PUNISHMENT**
4. **COMMENTS**

EZEKIEL 8:5-18
King James Version

Then said he unto me, Son of man, lift up thine eyes now the way toward the north. So I lifted up mine eyes the way toward the north, and behold northward at the gate of the altar this **image of jealousy** in the entry. He said furthermore unto me, Son of man, seest thou what they do? even the **great abominations** that the house of Israel committeth here, that I should go far off from my sanctuary? but turn thee yet again, and thou shalt see **greater abominations**. And he brought me to the door of the court; and when I looked, behold a hole in the wall. Then said he unto me, Son of man, dig now in the wall: and when I had digged in the wall, behold a door. And he said unto me, Go in, and behold the **wicked abominations** that they do here. So I went in and saw; and behold **every form of creeping things, and abominable beasts**, and **all the idols** of the house of Israel, portrayed upon the wall round about. And there stood before them seventy men of the ancients of the house of Israel, and in the midst of them stood Jaazaniah the son of Shaphan, with **every man his censer in his hand**, and a thick cloud of **incense** went up. then said he unto me, Son of man, hast thou seen what the ancients of the house of Israel do in the dark, every man in the **chambers of his imagery**? for they say, The LORD seeth us not; The LORD hasth forsaken the earth. He said also unto me, turn thee yet again, and thou shalt see **greater abominations** that they do. Then he brought me to the door of the gate of the LORD's house which was toward the north; and behold, there sat **women weeping for Tammuz**. Then said he unto me, Hast thou see this, O son of man? turn thee yet again, and thou shalt see **greater abominations** than these. And he brought me into the inner court of the LORD's house, and behold, at the door of the temple of the LORD, between the porch and the altar, were about five and twenty men, with their backs toward the temple of the LORD, and their faces toward the east; and they **worshipped the sun toward the east**. Then he said unto me, Hast thou seen this, O son of man? Is it a light thing to the house of Judah that they commit the **abominations** which they commit here? **for they have filled the land with violence, and have returned to provoke me to anger: and lo, they put the branch to their nose. Therefore will I also deal in fury: mine eye shall not spare, neither will I have pity: and though they cry in mine ears with a loud voice, yet will I not hear them.**

Amplified Version

Then He (the Spirit) said to me, Son of man, now lift up your eyes to the north. So I lifted up my eyes toward the north, and behold, on the north of the altar gate was that **idol (image) of jealousy** in the entrance. Furthermore, (the Spirit) said to me, Son of man, do you see what they are doing? the **great abominations** that the house of Israel is committing here to drive Me far from My sanctuary? But you shall again see **greater abominations**. And He brought me to the door of the court; and when I looked, behold, there was a hole in the wall. then He said to me, Son of man, dig now in the wall. And when I had dug in the wall, behold, there was a door. And He said to me, Go in and see the **wicked abominations** that they do here. So I went in and saw there **pictures of every form of creeping things and loathsome beasts** and **all the idols** of the house of Israel, **painted round about on the wall**. And there stood before these **(pictures)** seventy men of the elders of the house of Israel, and in the midst of them stood Jaazaniah the son of Shaphan (the scribe), with **every man his censer in his hand**, and a thick cloud of **incense** was going up **(in prayer to these their Gods)**. Then said He to me, Son of man, have you seen what the elders of the house of Israel do in the dark, **every man in his (secret) chambers of (idol) pictures**? For they say, The Lord does not see us; the Lord has forsaken the land. He also said to me, Yet again you shall see **greater abominations** which they are committing. Then He brought me to the entrance of the north gate of the Lord's house; and behold, there sat **women weeping for Tammuz (a Babylonian God, who was supposed to die annually and subsequently be resurrected)**. Then said (the Spirit) to me, Have you seen this, O son of man? Yet gain you shall see **greater abominations** that they are committing. And He brought me to the inner court of the Lord's house; and behold at the door of the temple of the Lord, between the porch and the bronze altar, were about twenty-five men with their backs to the temple of the Lord and their faces toward the east, and **they were bowing themselves toward the east and worshiping the sun**. Then (the Spirit) said to me, Have you seen this, O son of man? Is it too slight a thing to the house of Judah to commit the **abominations** which they commit here, that **they must fill the land with violence and turn back afresh to provoke Me to anger? and behold, they put the branch to their nose (actually, before their mouths, in superstitious worship)! Therefore I will deal in wrath; My eye will not spare, nor will I have pity; and though they cry in My ears with a loud voice yet will I not hear them.**

IDOLATRY
Idol (image) of jealousy, great abominations, greater abominations, wicked abominations, pictures of every form of creeping things and loathsome beasts, all the idols, painted round about on the wall, (pictures), every man his censer in his hand, incense, (in prayer to these their Gods), every man in his (secret) chambers of (idol) pictures, greater abominations, women weeping for Tammuz (a Babylonian God, who was supposed to die annually and subsequently be resurrected), greater abominations, they were bowing themselves toward the east and worshiping the sun, abominations.

PUNISHMENT
They must fill the land with violence and turn back afresh to provoke Me to anger? and behold, they put the branch to their nose (actually, before their mouths, in superstitious worship)! Therefore I will deal in wrath; My eye will not spare, nor will I have pity; and though they cry in My ears with a loud voice yet will I not hear them.

COMMENTS

The abominations become greater and more wicked, these things were done in God's sanctuary, and the people were imagining worship of other Gods. They were worshiping idols, insects, beasts and planets. Here is a good example of people worshiping **pictures** of every form of creeping things and loathsome beasts, and **idols. You should not use incense because it is used in worship of other Gods. If we show interest in or attention to things that are not Godly, we are using a form of worship of other Gods; examples are ungodly holidays.** Could you say that there was Godly jealousy over what was going in the sanctuary?

REFERENCE

Deliverance Manual, Gene and Earline Moody, Deliverance Ministries

SECTION 8 - FEMALE CURSES

CONTENTS
1.   ISAIAH 3:16-26
    1. King James Version
    2. Amplified Version
2.   ANALYSIS OF SCRIPTURE
3.   COMMENTS
4.   MINISTRY

ISAIAH 3:16-26
King James Version

Moreover the LORD saith, <u>Because the daughters of Zion are haughty, and walk with stretched forth necks and wanton eyes, walking and mincing as they go, and making a tinkling with their feet</u>: Therefore the Lord will smite with a scab the crown of the head of the daughters of Zion, and the LORD will discover their secret parts. In that day the Lord will take away the bravery of their tinkling ornaments about their feet, and their cauls, and their round tires like the moon. The chains, and the bracelets, and the mufflers, The bonnets, and the ornaments of the legs, and the headbands, and the tablets, and the earrings, The rings, and nose jewels, The changeable suits of apparel, and the mantles, and the wimples, and the crisping pins, The glasses, and the fine linen, and the hoods, and the vails. And it shall come to pass, that instead of sweet smell there shall be stink; and instead of a girdle a rent; and instead of well set hair baldness; and instead of a stomacher a girding of sackcloth; and burning instead of beauty. Thy men shall fall by the sword, and thy mighty in the war. And her gates shall lament and mourn; and she being desolate shall sit upon the ground.

Amplified Version

Moreover, the Lord said, <u>Because the daughters of Zion are haughty and walk with outstretched necks and with undisciplined (flirtatious and alluring) eyes, tripping along with mincing and affected gait, and making a tinkling noise with (the anklets on) their feet</u>, Therefore the Lord will smite with a scab the crown of the heads of the daughters of Zion (making them bald), and the Lord will cause them to be (taken as captives and to suffer the indignity of being) stripped naked. In the day the Lord will take away the finery of their tinkling anklets, the caps of network, the crescent head ornaments, The pendants, the bracelets or chains, and the spangled face veils and scarves, The headbands, the short ankle chains (attached from one foot to the other to insure a measured gait), the sashes, the perfume boxes, the amulets or charms (suspended from the ears or neck), the signet rings and nose rings, The festal robes, the cloaks, the stoles and shawls, and the handbags, The hand mirrors, the fine lines (undergarments), the turbans, and the (whole body-enveloping) veils. And it shall come to pass that instead of the sweet odor of spices there shall be the stench of rottenness; and instead of a girdle, a rope; and instead of well-set hair, baldness; and instead of a rich robe, a girding of sackcloth; and searing (of captives by the scorching heat) instead of beauty. Your men shall fall by the sword, and your mighty men in battle. And (Jerusalem's) gates shall lament and mourn (as those who wail for the dead); and she, being ruined and desolate, shall sit upon the ground.

ANALYSIS OF SCRIPTURE
The scripture is very descriptive. In the sight of God, the women have sinned. They and their men, and the nation will be severely punished.

Because the daughters of Zion are haughty and walk with outstretched necks and with undisciplined (flirtatious and alluring) eyes, tripping along with mincing and affected gait, and making a tinkling noise with (the anklets on) their feet. This was the sin of the women.

The Lord will smite with a scab the crown of the heads of the daughters of Zion (making them bald), and the Lord will cause them to be (taken as captives and to suffer the indignity of being) stripped naked. In the day the Lord will take away the finery of their tinkling anklets, the caps of network, the crescent head ornaments, The pendants, the bracelets or chains, and the spangled face veils and scarves, The headbands, the short ankle chains (attached from one foot to the other to insure a measured gait), the sashes, the perfume boxes, the amulets or charms (suspended from the ears or neck), the signet rings and nose rings, The festal robes, the cloaks, the stoles and shawls, and the handbags, The hand mirrors, the fine lines (undergarments), the turbans, and the (whole body-enveloping) veils. And it shall come to pass that instead of the sweet odor of spices there shall be the stench of rottenness; and instead of a girdle, a rope; and instead of well-set hair, baldness; and instead of a rich robe, a girding of sackcloth; and searing (of captives by the scorching heat) instead of beauty. This is the punishment of the women.

Your men shall fall by the sword, and your mighty men in battle. And (Jerusalem's) gates shall lament and mourn (as those who wail for the dead); and she, being ruined and desolate, shall sit upon the ground. This is the punishment of the men, city and women.

COMMENTS
The women suffer physical ailments of baldness (scabs on the crowns of the heads) and stench of rottenness (probably female cancer of their private parts). The women suffer emotional ailments of indignity (nakedness, shame, embarrassment and having their finery taken away).

The men and nation also suffer because of the sins of their wives. God apparently holds the husbands responsible for the wives' actions. The husbands are the spiritual authorities of the wives. God holds everyone responsible: wives, husbands and nation.

If a woman is getting bald or has a skin disease on the head, or has female cancer of the private parts (especially the lower part of the body), there may be a spiritual roots to the diseases (sins opened the doors).

MINISTRY
Take the woman through deliverance and then pray for healing of the diseases.

SECTION 9 - CURSES OF APOSTATE CHURCH
(A Compassionate Roar)

CONTENTS
1. WHAT IS THE APOSTATE CHURCH?
2. IT IS ABOUT SELF!
4. WHAT DOES THE FUTURE HOLD?
4. WHAT IS SEXUAL SIN?
5. WHAT IS SIN?
6. REFERENCE

WHAT IS THE APOSTATE CHURCH?

Characteristics of the apostate church are: success-promising, user-friendly, prosperity and money-focused; programs, church calendars, and contemporary music and worship; motivational speakers; those who honor, practice and remain silent; and soporific pep-talks. Men will not put up with sound doctrine, and teachers who say what their itching ears want to hear. Do not believe that God will judge America. Church problems: timorous accommodating attitude, morally ambivalent preachers, fashion, position,

superficial, mute prophets, professional preachers and Christians, whitewash, ego-driven ministry, superficiality, charade, spiritual treachery and treason, psychobabble, shallowness, idolatry, seduction, covetous, greedy, pious activity, worldly accommodation, religious pride, apathy, materialism, crowds, growth, neglect of prayer, moral evils, doctrinal corruptions, happiness, earthly benefits, fads, religious humanism, triumphantism, another gospel, falsity, fraudulent compassion, charlatans, new teachings, celebrity,

fill meetings and pocketbooks, convenience, power and pleasure, success slogans, so-called moves of God, power religion, prosperity, positive mental images, pop psychology, other winds of doctrine, moralism, pragmatism, entertainment, competition, materialism, love of money, intellectual depravity, muting scriptural truth, lavish style of Christianity, distort truth, amoral, false prophets, blindly alter perception of truth, cowardly clergy and liberal church.

Have God's justice, exposure of sin, warnings of judgment, compassionate calls to repentance, the Cross, sin, accountability and eternal damnation omitted? Are we holding back God's message? Are we casual Christians? Do we ignore repentance, redemption, justice, righteousness, cleansing, right living, defending the fatherless and widow, holiness, wrath, accountability, repentance, death, wrath and other parts of The Bible.?

A UNITED METHODIST CHURCH
(The Homosexual Agenda)

The minister refused to conduct legal marriages until the denomination's ban on same-sex marriages was overturned. The church was described as members from diverse backgrounds exploring the many ways of understanding God, celebrating the gifts of all persons regardless of sexual orientation or gender identity, honoring a diversity of theological expressions, using both feminine and masculine images of God. Creed is a diversity of theological expressions: traditional Christianity, an appreciation of other sacred texts, concern for ecological dimensions of the creation and planet, Liberation theology, Native American spirituality, and a critique of patriarchal religion and hierarchy.

IT IS ABOUT SELF!

It is about self: self-deceptions, self-image, self-esteem, self-love, self-help programs, self-deluded, self-made fantasy, self-righteousness, self-destruction, self-absorption, selfish, **and many others.**

WHAT DOES THE FUTURE HOLD?

Is God bringing remedial judgment on America for our national iniquities? Remedial judgments are to shake us up to get us to listen. What consequences do we face: the ultimate death of our society, another 9/11, national tragedy, war, economic disintegration, natural disasters or a combination of these? Do we rival Sodom with our terrible evil and judgment-deserving nation, low standard of morals and our grievous sins? Are we heading for virtually abandoning restraint in the sin of America, bloodshed of killing our unborn, sexual licentiousness, gross immorality, pride and other public sins? Is our house burning? Are we at the abyss of judgement? Are we barbarians?

God is exceedingly angry with America. America, as a nation, is ripe for destruction, and certain judgement. We have a window of mercy which the Church had better utilize.

WHAT IS SEXUAL SIN?

Sexual sin is one of the biggest problems in and out of the Church. Abortion is shedding of innocent blood, officially sanctioned public-approved ritualized human sacrifice against the helpless, defenseless and weak, the right of a woman to her own body, every child should be wanted, the viability of the fetus, the right to choose, abortion clinics; sexual license in movies, TV and music; fatherlessness; same-sex couples adopting children; immorality, child molestation, rape, homosexual perversion,

pornography, sexual libertines, gay rights activists, sex education debauchery, AIDS, pornography, heterosexual fornication and adultery, pornography, sensuality, killing our unborn, teaching our children to accept sin, pervasive immorality, fornication, adultery, sodomy, same-sex marriage, pro-choice, gross sexual perversion, licentiousness, sensual pleasure, sexual license, whoremongering, adoption of children by homosexuals and lust.

WHAT IS SIN?

According to The Bible, sin has many forms: pride, tolerance, non-judgmental, physician-assisted suicide, presumptuous sins, depravity of society, situational ethics, instant gratification, adoption of children by homosexuals, national hypocrisy, lying, worldliness, covetousness, bitterness and hostility, drug addictions and other evils, sewer of sin, violence; feticide, animals treated more humanely than humans, abusing children, violence in our streets and schools, wife-beating, mugging, robbery, murder, parricide, feminists and New Agers in schools, drug epidemic, euthanasia, aggressive sinning, evil, decay, degeneracy, foolish, arrogance, contempt, corrupt, profane, reprobate, debased, compromise, rebellion, bondage, seared conscious, brainwash, suicide, homicidal atrocities, indifferent, hardened, bold sinning, lukewarm, brazen, detestable, spiritual drought, apathetic, degrading passions, moral impurity, Corinthian immorality and situational ethics.

REFERENCE

A Compassionate Roar - Raising An Urgent Voice In Our Window Of Mercy by John O. Anderson, Bridge Logos

SECTION 10 - CURSE OF PRIDE

CONTENTS
1. **SCRIPTURES**
    1. Pride Scriptures
    2. Other Pride Scriptures
    3. Proud Scriptures
    4. Other Proud Scriptures
    5. Proudly Scriptures
    6. Other Proudly Scriptures
    7. Humble Scriptures
    8. Other Humble Scriptures
2. **SPIRITUAL**
3. **EXAMPLES**
4. **PROBLEMS**
5. **PRAYER**
6. **LIST OF DEMONS**
7. **GOD HATES PRIDE**
8. **PRAYER OF REPENTANCE FROM PRIDE**
9. **REFERENCES**

SCRIPTURES

Prov. 6:16-19 **These six things doth THE LORD hate: yea, seven are an <u>abomination</u> unto him: <u>A proud look</u>, a lying tongue, and hands that shed innocent blood, An heart that deviseth wicked imaginations, feet that be swift in running to mischief, A false witness that speaketh lies, and he that soweth discord among brethren.**

Pride Scriptures

Lev. 26:19 I will break the pride of your power.
Ps. 10:2 The wicked in his pride.
Ps. 10:4 Through the pride of his countenance.
Ps. 73:6 Therefore pride compasseth them about.
Prov. 8:13 Pride, and arrogance, and the evil way.
Prov. 11:2 When pride cometh, then cometh shame.
Prov. 13:10 Only by pride cometh contention.
Prov. 14:3 Of the foolish is a rod of pride.
Prov. 16:18 Pride goeth before destruction.
Prov. 29:23 A man's pride shall bring him low.
Mk. 7:22 An evil eye, blasphemy, pride.
I Ti. 3:6 Lest being lifted up with pride.
I Jn. 2:16 The pride of life.

God will break your power, bring shame and destruction, and bring you low for your pride. Characteristics are wicked, countenance, surrounds, arrogance, evil, contention, foolish, evil eye, blasphemy, lifted up and pride of life.

Other Pride Scriptures

I Sa. 17:28; II Chr. 32:26; **Job 33:17, 35:25 and 41:15,34;** Ps. 10:2,4, 31:20, 36:11, 59:12 and 73:6; **Prov. 6:16-19, 8:13, 11:2, 13:10, 14:3, 16:18 and 29:23;** Is. 9:9, 16:6, 23:9, 25:11 and 28:1,3; **Jer. 13:9,17, 48:29 and 49:16;** Eze. 7:10, 16:49,56 and 30:6; **Dan. 4:37 and 5:20;** Hos. 5:5 and 7:10; Obad. 3; **Zeph. 2:10, 3:11, 9:6, 10:11 and 11:3;** Zec. 9:6, 10:11 and 11:3; Mark 7:22, 1 Tim. 3:6, 1 John 2:16

Characteristics are naughtiness, **pride of thine heart,** hide pride, pride of evil men, children of pride, pride of man, foot of pride, taken in their pride, **pride of various nations,** haughtiness, stain the pride, bring down their pride, crown of pride, mar the pride, great pride, weep for your pride, arrogance, pride hath budded, iniquity of pride, pride of power, walk in pride, hardened in pride, rejoice in thy pride, cut off the pride, and pride is spoiled.

Proud Scriptures

Job 9:13 The proud helpers do stoop (bow) under him.
Job 26:12 He smiteth through the proud.
Job 40:11 And behold every one that is proud.
Job 40:12 Look on every one that is proud.
Ps. 12:3 The tongue that speaketh proud things.
Ps. 31:23 Plentifully rewardeth the proud doer.
Ps. 40:4 Trust, and respecteth not the proud.
Ps. 86:14 The proud are risen against me.
Ps. 94:2 Render a reward to the proud.
Ps. 101:5 A proud heart will not I suffer.
Ps. 119:21 Rebuked the proud that are cursed.
Ps. 119:51 The proud have had me greatly in derision.
Ps. 119:69 The proud have forged a lie against me.
Ps. 119:78 Let the proud be ashamed.
Ps. 119:85 The proud have digged pits for me.
Ps. 119:122 Let not the proud oppress me.
Ps. 123:4 And with the contempt of the proud.
Ps. 138:6 But the proud he knoweth afar off.
Ps. 140:5 The proud have hid a snare for me.
Prov. 6:17 A proud look, a lying tongue.
Prov. 15:25 Will destroy the house of the proud.
Prov. 16:5 Every one that is proud in heart.
Prov. 16:19 To divide the spoil with the proud.
Prov. 21:4 A proud heart.
Prov. 21:24 Proud and haughty scorner is his name.
Prov. 21:24 Who dealeth in proud wrath.
Prov. 28:25 He that is of a proud heart.
Eccl. 7:8 Is better than the proud in spirit.
Is. 2:12 And he shall be brought low.
Is. 13:11 The arrogancy of the proud to cease.
Jer. 13:15 Be not proud.

Jer. 50:31 I am against thee, O thou most proud.
Jer. 50:32 The most proud shall stumble and fall.
Hab. 2:5 By wine, he is a proud man.
Mal. 3:15 And now we call the proud happy.
Mal. 4:1 And all the proud, yea.
Lk. 1:51 He hath scattered the proud.
Rom. 1:30 Haters of God, despiteful, proud.
I Ti. 6:4 He is proud, knowing nothing.
2 Ti. 3:2 Own selves, covetous, boasters, proud.
Jas. 4:6 He saith, God resisteth the proud.
1 Pet. 5:5 For God resisteth the proud.

God will smite, reward (punish), not respect, not suffer, rebuke, curse, shame, know afar off, be against, scatter, resist and destroy, bring low the house of the proud, and stoop (bow) the proud helpers. Characteristics are lying tongue, derision, lie, digged pits, oppress, contempt, snare, divide the spoil, haughty scorner, arrogancy, to cease, haters of God, despiteful, knowing nothing, covetous, boasters, and **proud look, heart, wrath, spirit and man.**

Other Proud Scriptures

Job 38:11, Ps. 124:5 and Is. 16:6, Jer. 43:2, 48:29 & 50:29. Characteristics are thy proud waves be stayed, the proud waters have gone over, he is very proud, all the proud men, he is exceeding proud, and she hath been proud.

Proudly Scriptures

Ex. 18:11 They dealt proudly, he was above them.
I Sa. 2:3 Talk no more so exceeding proudly.
Neh. 9:16 But they and our fathers dealt proudly.
Neh. 9:29 Yet they dealt proudly.
Ps. 17:10 With their mouth they speak proudly.
Ps. 31:18 Which speak grievous things proudly.
Is. 3:5 Himself proudly against the ancient.

God will be above those that deal proudly. Characteristics are grievous things, proudly against the ancient, and **exceeding, dealt and speak proudly.**

Other Proudly Scriptures

Neh. 9:10 and Obad. 12.

Characteristics are they dealth proudly against them and spoken proudly in the day of distress.

Humble Scriptures

Ex. 10:3 Refuse to humble.
Deut. 8:2 Humble - prove - know - keep.
2 Chron. 7:14 Humble - pray - seek - turn.
Job 22:29 Save the humble person.

Psa. 9:12 Cry of the humble.
Prov. 29:23 Honour shall uphold the humble.
Isa. 57:15 Contrite and humble spirit.
Matt. 18:4 The same is the greatest in kingdom of Heaven.
James 4:6 Giveth grace to the humble.
1 Peter 5:5-6 Be clothed with humility.

You should humble yourself before GOD. Humble is the opposite of pride. **Clearly GOD will honor those that are humble before Him and put down the proud.**

Other Humble Scriptures
Deut. 8:16; Jud. 19:24; 2 Chron. 34:27; Psa. 10:2 & 17, 34:2, 69:32; Prov. 6:3, 16:19; Jer. 13:18; Matt. 23:12; 2 Cor. 12:21; and James 4:10.

Characteristics are humble thee, humble maiden, tender heart, wicked pride, humble desire, humble shall hear, be glad, humble thyself, humble spirit, humble be exalted and humble me.

You could also search the word humble (24) and its derivatives: humbled (25), humbledst (1), humbleness (1), humbleth (6) and humbly (2) for a total of fifty-nine times.

SPIRITUAL
Spiritual pride, ego and vanity are large hindrances to living your Christian life. Pride, ego and vanity can affect your secular life. All forms of pride can affect many areas in your walk with God and living your secular life for the worse.

Remember that pride comes before loss of power, shame, contention, destruction, being brought low, an evil eye and blasphemy. It comes before a fall from your position in Christ or the world.

Pride can come in the ministry of deliverance to those who are hurt, bruised and wounded. When you learn that you have power over the enemy, you can become exalted in your thoughts about your self (Luke 10:17-**20**). This is a ministry of signs, wonders and miracles but they are being done by the Power of God working through you. You can't do anything without God.

There are many types of religious spirits that affect Christianity. Religious spirits are given freedom due to the way you think about religion. These will be found in the ways that Christians fight against each other due to differences in beliefs. Christians fight against each other even in the same church due to ungodly reasons.

Pride can especially affect the leaders who think the credit for what God is doing belongs to them (Proverbs 6:16-19). When we fall into pride, we can't think correctly and make errors in judgement.

Pride can affect the Christian marriage. Are you following Eph. 5:22 & 25 and 6:1 & 4 for the perfect family before God? It would be good for you to read Eph. 5:22-6:4 for a more complete explanation.

EXAMPLES

I believe that The Book Of Ester, Chapters 3-7 contain the best example of pride in the Bible. Mordecai would not bow or reverence Haman. Haman had his pride hurt and was full of wrath. Haman obtained a decree to destroy Mordecai and the Jews. Haman was hanged on his own gallows.

There are many other examples of pride. The word pride is used forty-six times in The King James Version. **Clearly GOD hates pride and it is an abomination to Him. GOD will dishonor those that have pride.** As Christians, I believe that GOD hates pride because we are taking credit for what He has done.

How about Satan's fall from Heaven (Isa. 14:4-23 and Eze. 28:11-19)? Satan took a third of the angels with him who fell because of pride. There are other examples of pride in The Bible and what it cost those who fell into Satan's trap.

PROBLEMS

Pride is a huge sea-serpent demon coiled in abdomen who dislikes Psa. 74:13-14. Pride uses logic, rationalization and justification to know things of God; distracts and disturbs concentration in Bible study and prayer; causes weariness and sleepiness in worship services (Job 41, Isa. 27:1); blocks mind and hinders spiritual growth. Pride causes mourning, spiritual darkness, arrogance, spiritual pride; ego, little pride, brooding, melancholy, depression, gloominess, mental dejection, irascibility;

Orion: first lieutenant of Lucifer, controls counterfeit gifts, false peace and piety; enters with any compromise of the Word of God; very proud, beautiful and intellectual spirit.

Prince Charming: Attacks ministers, especially those in deliverance. Uses pride to restrict the ministry to a specific area or to certain people. Will use pressure tactics to lead to radical modifications or abandonment of casting out evil spirits. Host of intellectual and philosophical spirits, religious spirits, false gifts to give a veneer of spirituality.

PRAYER

Almighty God, I come to you in the matter of pride. Pride is an abomination to you. I renounce pride and turn away from it. I humble myself before you and come to you as a little child. I ask you to forgive me and I forgive myself. I do this for sins committed in pride that would have affected me.

I forgive my ancestors, descendents, and anyone else that has had spiritual or carnal authority over me. I ask that you save them, bless them with spiritual blessings,

bring them into truth and meet their needs out of your riches in glory. I ask these things in the blessed name of Jesus Christ, Lord, Master and Savior. Amen.

LIST OF DEMONS
(Proper Names Of Demons)

Leviathan, King of the Children of Pride: (Job 41 and 104:16; Isa. 27:1) Using logic rather than being led by God; carnal justification to know the things of God; hinders spiritual growth; disturbs concentration in Bible study and prayer; weariness and sleepiness in worship services; and blocks mind. Causes pride, mourning, spiritual darkness, arrogance, spiritual pride, ego, little pride, rationalization, distracts, brooding, melancholy, depression, gloominess, mental dejection, irascibility, mourning, spiritual darkness, arrogance, ego.

Rahab: dragon, pride, **(Isa. 51:9-10)**.

Orion: compromise of the Word of God, counterfeit gifts, false peace, piety.

Prince Charming: intellectual and philosophical spirits, religious spirits, false gifts, veneer of spirituality.

Absalom: pride, vanity, rebellion, deception, seduction, treachery: mind idolatry, vanity, perfection, competition, schizophrenia, self righteousness, haughtiness, importance, arrogance, self deception, ego.

Mind Idolatry: pride, intellectualism, rationalization, ego.

Vanity: Belphegar, Belfagar, Apollyon, Scorpion, fears, Absalom, pride, Orion, perfection, schizophrenia.

Perfectionism: pride, vanity, frustration, irritability, intolerance, anger, criticism, schizophrenia.

Competition: pride, driving, argument, ego, compromise, indecision, blocked spiritual growth, Orion.

Schizophrenia: pride, etc.

Ego: mind idolatry, pride, perfection, competition, schizophrenia.

Carvar: spiritual destruction, under spirit of Lucifer.

Carbar: a ruler: spiritual blockage, blocks spiritual truth.

Reserpcarian, Rucipacerian, a controller: spirit and will, blocks spirit and will.

Additimus: blocks spiritual truth.

Markai, Markiah: blocks spiritual understanding, causes spiritual blindness.

Morondo: blocks reading of The Word, blocks spiritual light.

Remus, Remur: causes sleep in spiritual environment.

(See Self Righteousness, Haughtiness, Importance, Arrogance, Self Deception.)

GOD HATES PRIDE

These six things doth THE LORD hate: yea, seven are an abomination unto him: A proud look, a lying tongue and hands that shed innocent blood. An heart that deviseth wicked imaginations, feet that be swift in running to mischief. A false witness that speaketh lies and he that soweth discord among brethren.

The proud helpers do stoop (bow) under Him. He smiteth through the proud. Plentifully rewardeth the proud doer. Trust and respecteth not the proud. Render a reward to the proud. A proud heart will not I suffer. Let the proud be ashamed. But the proud He knoweth afar off. Will destroy the house of the proud. And he shall be brought low. I am against thee, O thou most proud. The most proud shall stumble and fall. He hath scattered the proud. He saith, God resisteth the proud. For God resisteth the proud. They dealt proudly, He was above them.

God will break your power, bring shame and destruction, and bring you low for your pride. God will smite, reward (punish), not respect, not suffer, rebuke, curse, shame, know afar off, be against, scatter, resist and destroy, bring low the house of the proud and stoop (bow) the proud helpers. God will be above those that deal proudly.

PRAYER OF REPENTANCE FROM PRIDE

Almighty God, I come to you in the matter of pride. Pride is an abomination to you. I renounce pride and turn away from it. I humble myself before you and come to you as a little child. I ask you to forgive me and I forgive myself. I do this for sins committed in pride that would have affected me. Amen PRIDE

These six things doth THE LORD hate: yea, seven are an abomination unto him: A proud look, a lying tongue and hands that shed innocent blood. An heart that deviseth wicked imaginations, feet that be swift in running to mischief. A false witness that speaketh lies and he that soweth discord among brethren.

The proud helpers do stoop (bow) under Him. He smiteth through the proud. Plentifully rewardeth the proud doer. Trust and respecteth not the proud. Render a reward to the proud. A proud heart will not I suffer. Let the proud be ashamed. But the proud He knoweth afar off. Will destroy the house of the proud. And he shall be brought low. I am against thee, O thou most proud. The most proud shall stumble and fall. He hath scattered the proud. He saith, God resisteth the proud. For God resisteth the proud. They dealt proudly, He was above them.

God will break your power, bring shame and destruction, and bring you low for your pride. God will smite, reward (punish), not respect, not suffer, rebuke, curse, shame, know afar off, be against, scatter, resist and destroy, bring low the house of the proud and stoop (bow) the proud helpers. God will be above those that deal proudly.

Almighty God, I come to you in the matter of pride. Pride is an abomination to you. I renounce pride and turn away from it. I humble myself before you and come to you as a little child. I ask you to forgive me and I forgive myself. I do this for sins committed in pride that would have affected me. Amen

REFERENCES
Proper Names Of Demons by Win Worley, WRW Publications, Lansing, IL

SECTION 11 - CURSES FOR SHEDDING INNOCENT BLOOD
(Written By Earline Moody)

CONTENTS
1. PREFACE
2. CAIN AND ABLE
3. MANASSEH
4. AHAB AND JEZEBEL
5. IDOL WORSHIP
6. AMERICA
7. AS A CHILD
8. TAKING A BRIBE
9. JESUS' CONDEMNATION
10. CHILD SACRIFICE
11. INNOCENT BLOOD
12. GENE'S COMMENTS
13. PRAYER
14. LIST OF DEMONS

PREFACE

I would like to examine the question of shedding innocent blood, or murder of innocent people. In the last twenty years there seems to be a great rise in the murder of innocent people or what seems like innocent people. Wondering why this has happened has set me to doing a little study. It seems that as the years go by unprovoked, or what looks like unprovoked, murders become more common.

I have read about so many murders in my town that I don't pay much attention to them anymore. I do find that I stay away from certain places and types of people. I wouldn't just go anywhere as I did as a child. I take my husband or someone else when I have to go to certain areas. We have a shopping center that I almost never go to alone because I consider it not to be safe even in the day time.

I started to notice a trend in our area; on the surface it seems **more women are being attacked and/or murdered than in years past**. I have often wondered why. I think we can find some answers in the Bible.

One thing we have learned in deliverance sessions; those people who get into the occult, drugs or sex have a very difficult time giving their old activities up. After much prayer and Bible study, it has become evident that since these are activities carried on in idol or Satan worship, the demons will really work on these people to get back in. It is far better and safer to leave idol and Satan worship out of you life. This means no sex before marriage, no desiring forbidden knowledge, no flirting with the occult, no use of illegal drugs, and no worship of anyone as Lord except Jesus Christ.

We have seen how rebellion, hate, envy and jealousy grow extremely rapidly. The Bible tells us to obey the instructions of God quickly and enthusiastically. Quickly forgive others, repent of rebellion and quickly correct any errors in your thinking.

Have you seen families or a person that seemed to never belong; never be able to make enough money to take care of themselves, let alone their families; families who seemed to always be despised in the neighborhood; those who work and make plenty of money but never seen to have enough; those who never seem to be able to come to Jesus; those who stay in their idolatry and witchcraft even when it is obvious they are gaining nothing but are being damned, etc.?

I have a new Bible which I have started to read from beginning to end, marking God's words in red. I came upon this verse, which I will have to admit, never registered with me before. **Whosoever sheds men's blood, by man shall his blood be shed; for in the image of God He made man** (Genesis 9:6). Since God created man in His image we should respect that which God gave honor to and not deface God's image, by unjustly killing a person. There is a law for killing by those who plan and carry out murder. **There is a curse on those magistrates who do not punish murders** (Rom. 13:4).

CAIN AND ABLE

The first account of innocent blood being shed in the Bible is in Genesis 4. The brothers Cain and Able have both offered sacrifice to God but only Able's is accepted. Cain becomes exceedingly angry and indignant. V.6, **And the Lord said to Cain, Why are you angry? And why do you look sad and dejected? V.7, If you do well, will you not be accepted? And if you do not well, sin crouches at your door; its desire is for you, and you must master it.**

Cain lets anger, rage, hate, jealousy take hold of him. Instead of repenting of disobedience to God's instruction concerning sacrifices, he decides to destroy the object of his anger. He murders his brother, hides the body, and pretends he doesn't know anything about it.

God is not deceived by this act, neither is the Devil. For God looks into Cain's heart and sees the evil there. Cain could have confessed his sin but he did not, instead he lies. V.11 contains his sentence. **And now you are cursed by reason of the earth, which has opened its mouth to receive you brother's (shed) blood from your hand.** V.12, **When you till the ground, it shall no longer yield to you its strength; you shall be a vagabond on the earth (in perpetual exile, a degraded outcast).** Even at this point Cain could have repented and been forgiven, but he would not. In fact, he was telling God that God would have to accept him because of his fine gift. There is nothing we can offer God fine enough to cause Him to accept us. It is only by accepting Jesus Christ as Saviour and afterward living by God's directions that we can be acceptable to God. Cain began to tell God about the harshness of his sentence. In the light of his murder of his brother, this attitude shows his opposition to God's laws. He should have considered his sentence light compared to the sentence he deserved.

MANASSEH

Moreover, Manasseh shed very much innocent blood, filling Jerusalem from one end to the other--besides his sin in making Judah sin, by doing evil in the sight of the Lord (II Kings 21:16). II Chron. 33:1-10, He burned his children as an offering to his God in the valley of Ben-hinnom.

Manasseh, evil son of good Hezekiah, not only worshiped other Gods but he put their images in God's Temple. Children were gifts from God given by Him to parents who then turned and killed them, and sacrificed them to demons. This was a terrible affront to God, a great rebellion, and a terrible sin which brings curses for many generations, possible forever, on a family line. It takes sincere repentance for these sins of self and/or ancestors.

The Lord sent against Jehoiakim bands of Chaldeans, of Syrians, of Moabites and of Ammonites. And He sent them to Judah to destroy it, according to the word of the Lord which He spoke by His prophets. Surely this came upon Judah at the commandant of the Lord, to remove them out of His sight because of the sins of Manasseh according to all the sins he had done, And also for the innocent blood that he shed. For he filled Jerusalem with innocent blood, and the Lord would not pardon (II Kings 24:2-4).

Jehoiakim was a descendent of Manasseh; the sins of his father he did plus he received the punishment and curses of his father. Good King Hezekiah prayed to not die, God heard him, and he proceeded to give Israel the worst king it had had so far. (Read of ten tragic results from God giving Hezekiah what he wanted so badly, II Kings 20:18; 21:1, 3-4, 6, 9, 14, 16, 20.) It was good that Hezekiah prayed earnestly but at the end of giving his desire list to God, he should have submitted himself to God's plan.

Josiah, son of Manasseh, did right in the sight of the Lord and God stayed His wrath until Josiah died. But Manasseh's grandson, Jehoiakim, followed after Manasseh and great was the destruction on Judah.

There is a good possibility we would never have heard of Nebuchadnezzar, if it had not been for the Kings of Judah going after other Gods and shedding innocent blood. God appointed him to be king, and to take into captivity Judah and the rest of the known world.

AHAB AND JEZEBEL

I Kings 21-22 and II Kings 10, You will see an example of the results of shedding innocent blood on Ahab's household. Ahab wanted to have the vineyard of Naboth. Naboth refused to sell. Ahab came into his house, jumped into bed, whined around and pouted until he manipulated Jezebel to solve his problem. She had Naboth framed and killed. God issued the results of that curse. V.19, **where the dogs licked the blood of Naboth shall they also lick your blood** (To Ahab). V.21, **I will bring evil on you and utterly sweep away and cut off from Ahab every male, bond and free** (To Ahab's sons). V.23, **the dogs will eat Jezebel by the wall of Jezreel** (To Jezebel). These things happened just as God said.

IDOL WORSHIP

Jer.2:34, This is a good chapter to read completely. God, through the prophets, is telling the history of sin to these people. He reminds them that He brought them out of Egypt and set them free. They have forgotten His care and provisions in the wilderness, and being brought into a lane of plenty. Not even the priests ask for the Lord. The rulers transgressed against God, and the prophets prophesied by the authority of and in the name of Baal. Then God tells them what they are like and what will come upon them. He likens them to **restless females in heat looking for a male**. In verses 35-37 He explains how vain and hopeless their worship of idols is, and what destruction they have brought upon themselves.

In their idol worship **they burn their babies and sacrifice their children**; they also kill the innocent poor. V.34 tells them they have done these things because of their lust for idolatry.

AMERICA

This group of verses should serve to **warn us in America of much horror, sadness and distress ahead. I try to imagine what terror a baby goes through when it is murdered.** It can be nothing but murder. We can see how far we have fallen when we pick to murder those who are unable to do anything to defend themselves. See also Jer. 22:3,17; 26:15.

There will be judgement coming on our land for the guilt of the innocent blood that has been shed on our soil. These are some of the consequences we can expect: the above and those things we read about happening to the Old Testament people.

There must be sincere and deep repentance for the agreement to or the act of murder of innocents. **If you give consent to abortion, you are also guilty.** When Daniel asked God to forgive the sins of his nation, he used the terms us not them. Maybe we should do that too.

AS A CHILD

As a child on a mountain in Tennessee, we heard of murder only once. It was a great shock to us. Nothing like this had ever happened in my lifetime before. It took us children a long time to feel safe to go and come as we had before. There were no more murders there that I heard about, so in time, we became trusting again and went about alone without fear.

TAKING A BRIBE

Ps. 10:8, In this chapter we get a good picture of **the wicked person who plots and plans murder of innocents. He is** greedy, full of pride, persecutes the poor, spurns, renounces and despises the Lord, refuses to heed God's instructions and warnings, thinks he will never be punished, his ways are grievous, he believes he will never have adversity or want, his mouth is full of cursing, deceit, oppression and fraud, trouble and sin are under his tongue, and he ambushes and slays the poor and innocent.

Ps. 15:5 tells us that those who will take a bribe to slay the innocent will not dwell in the tabernacle and in God's Holy Hill.

Cursed is he who takes a bribe to slay an innocent person, all the people shall say, Amen (Deut. 27:25). **This will include all parties participating in abortion of unborn children:** the father, mother, doctor, nurses and others who agree to the abortion. It includes those who are bribed to lie or kill, and judges who accept bribes to cancel sentences or give light sentences to those who have committed murder or have lied to protect the guilty.

JESUS' CONDEMNATION

Matt. 27:4, When Judas saw that Jesus was condemned to be killed; his remorse was little more than a selfish dread of the consequences of betraying innocent blood. It looks like Judas didn't have the courage to face his friends after betraying Jesus. I'm sure he knew what he had done.

Matt. 27:24, Even Pilot wanted everyone to know he was not responsible for the innocent blood of Jesus. V.25, **Then answered all the people, and said His blood be on us, and on our children.** Once when we were working in deliverance with a person of Hebrew blood inheritance, we were impressed to have them repent for this curse and break it. They then began to shake and tremble violently. When they were free of these spirits, the shaking stopped.

CHILD SACRIFICE

And served their idols, which were a snare to them. Yes,, they sacrificed their sons and their daughters to demons (Ps. 106:36-42). And shed innocent blood, even the blood of their sons and their daughters, whom they sacrificed to the idols of Canaan; and the land was polluted with blood. Thus were they defiled by their own works, and played the harlot and practiced idolatry with their own deeds of idolatrous rites. Therefore the wrath of the Lord was kindled against His people, insomuch that He abhorred and rejected His own heritage (II Kings 16:3.). And He gave them into the hand of the heathen nations, and they that hated them ruled over them. Their enemies also oppressed them, and they were brought into subjection under the hand of their foes (Deut. 32:17).

Because the people have forsaken Me, and have estranged and profaned this place (Jerusalem), by burning incense in it to other Gods that neither they nor their fathers nor the kings of Judah have known; and because they have filled this place with the blood of innocents, and have built the high places of Baal to burn their sons in the fire for burnt offerings to Baal, which I commanded not, nor spoke it, nor did it come into My mind or heart; Therefore, behold, the days are coming, says the Lord, when this place shall no more be called Topheth, or the Valley of Ben-hinnom, but the Valley of Slaughter. I will cause their people to fall by the sword of their enemies, and by the hand of those who seek their life; and their dead bodies will I give to be food for the birds of the air and for the beasts of the earth. I will make this city to be an astonishment and a horror and a hissing; I will cause them to eat the flesh of their sons and their daughters, and neighbors because of the distress of their life (Jer. 19:4-9).

INNOCENT BLOOD

See these scriptures on shedding innocent blood: **Keep very far from a false matter and (be very careful) not to condemn to death the innocent and the righteous, for I will not justify and acquit the wicked** (Ex. 23:7).

Lest innocent blood be shed in your land, which the Lord your God gives you as an inheritance, and so blood guilt be upon you (Deut. 19:10).

In the verses just before this one, God is setting up cities of refuge for those who accidentally kill another. God did not want the avenger of blood to kill while he was hot with anger. (If the avenger killed one who had accidentally killed, then the avenger would be guilty of shedding innocent blood.) The one who had accidentally killed another could stay in the city of refuge until the elders of his city could determine if he was guilty of hating and planning to kill. If it was certain that he hated and planned to kill, then they would go into the city of refuge and bring him out and slay him.

Why do this? V.13, **Your eyes shall not pity him, but you shall clear Israel of the guilt of innocent blood, that it may be well with you.**

This is the provision for redeeming the land where one is found murdered and no one knows who did the murder. Deut. 21:1-9, If one is found slain in open land, then the city nearest to the body shall bring a heifer to a valley never sown, break it's neck, and there the men from the city would wash their hands and say whether they had seen the murder or done it.

V.8, **Forgive, O Lord, Your people Israel, whom You have redeemed, and do not allow the shedding of innocent blood to be charged to Your people Israel. And the guilt of the blood shall be forgiven them. V.9, So shall you purge the guilt of innocent blood from among you, when you do what is right in the sight of the Lord.**

Cursed is he who slays his neighbor secretly. All the people shall say, Amen (Deut. 27:24). Even if you should never get caught, you and your descendents will be under a curse and will be hunted by others and be killed. The Devil will never leave you and your descendents alone until you repent of your sins, accept Jesus as Saviour, break the curses on the family line, cast out the demons, and live according to the Bible thereafter. If you or you children sin in this manner later, the curse will return.

I Sam. 19:5, Saul had ordered David slain but Jonathan attempted to persuade Saul to stop before he shed innocent blood. Why was Jonathan concerned? We will see that the curse for shedding innocent blood would effect Jonathan and Saul's descendents, especially the males.

Ps. 94:21, There are those who band together to condemn the innocent to death, but the Lord will turn their own iniquity back upon them.

Six things the Lord hates: A proud look, a lying tongue, and <u>hands that shed innocent blood</u>, a heart that manufactures wicked thoughts and plans, feet that are swift in running to evil, A false witness who breaths out lies (even under oath), and he who sows discord among the brethren (Pro. 6:17-19).

Their feet run to evil, and they make hast to shed innocent blood; their thoughts are thoughts are of iniquity; desolation and destruction are in their paths and highways. The way of peace they know not, and there is no justice or right in their goings; they have made them crooked paths; whoever goes in them knows not peace (Isa. 59:7-8).

Ezekiel 13 tells us about people who are occult taking bribes to keep alive those who should die, and to kill those who should live. God says in verse 23 that He will deliver His people out of their hand. In Chapter 14, God explains what He will do to those who worship idols and still come around asking for God's advice. He will be cut off from the midst of My people. God says that when **the land sins (which is like our law allowing and financing abortion), He will stretch out His hand against it** and cut off their bread, send famine, and cut off from it man and beast. And that even if Noah, Daniel and Job were in that land, they could save only themselves by their own uprightness. You and I will stand before God on our own record and will not be able to make claims of rightness because of what our families have done.

From this scripture we have learned: it is a very severe thing to take the life of any human being. **It is most severe to take the life of the innocent, the unborn** or the poor. To murder the unborn in a attempt to cover other sins only gets a person in more trouble that having the child.

GENE'S COMMENTS

It is very clear that those participating in sexual sins (which lead to pregnancy) and then a decision is made to have an abortion are committing murder. The murder of an innocent child then opens the parents to demon attacks of being murdered or having violence committed against them.

A couple that does not want a child should use birth control methods that prevent pregnancy. This is better than having an abortion of an unwanted child. Single parents should not deliberately have children outside of marriage. They are cursed and their descendents are cursed to the tenth generation.

After having an abortion, the woman is subject to having miscarriages or not being able to get pregnant again. She may have painful and prolonged bleeding, and pain during her menstrual cycles. **She is subjected to many cruel emotions such as paranoia and insecurity.**

Rape can lead to pregnancy. Do you have a right before God to kill the child because you were raped? Soul ties should be broken with any sexual partners outside of marriage whether by rape or by sexual consent.

The church is drastically affected by the bastard which is a child conceived out of wedlock. The bastards have great difficulty in going to church and participating in the church services. Those who have sexual demons may act religious in church to cover their guilt about their sexual sins.

PRAYER

Dear Father in Heaven, there are curses that fall on individuals, families, races and nations for the sin of shedding innocent blood. This is a curse that travels down the family line. I ask for forgiveness for myself and those before me who have sinned against you and others by shedding innocent blood.

We have greatly erred in shedding innocent blood in the United States. Lord forgive us of this terrible sin, redeem us from quilt and cleanse the land.

I repent of having become involved in acts that show worship and obedience to the Devil and his demons. I repent of occult acts: worship, drugs, sex, thievery, murder, etc. I break soul ties with others that I practiced these acts with.

You have given us power over the power of the Devil. I break the curse of shedding innocent blood off my family and my descendents in the name of Jesus Christ. I break curses of idol worship, Satanism and illicit sex in Jesus name.

You have said that if I call on the name of the Lord I can be delivered. I call upon the name of the Lord Jesus Christ to set me free. I thank you Jesus for all you have done for me. I commit my life to you in a greater way today than I have before. Please instruct me, help me to correct my life and bring it into subjection to You. I pray this prayer in the name of Jesus Christ, God's son. Amen.

LIST OF DEMONS

Related lists of demons include **Bastards**, **Effeminacy - Sins of Sodom**, **Rape**, **Sexual Harassment - Abuse - Assault - Violence**, and **Sexual Sin and Diseases** which can be found in **Mass Deliverance Manual**.

We come against demons associated with shedding innocent blood, murder of innocent people, and sacrificing children to demons and idols of sex. We come against spirits of anger, sadness, dejection, rage, hate, envy, jealousy, pretense, falseness, bribery, lying, killing, rebellion, Jezebel and Ahab, greed, pride, cursing, deceit, fraud, oppression, Baal and other sexual idols, lust, combination of occult, illicit drugs and sex, seeking forbidden knowledge, burning incense, worship of sex, terror, cowardliness, idolatry, witchcraft, thievery, murder, Satanism and other related demon families. We come against Asmodeous and other marriage breaking spirits.

SECTION 12 - INCEST AND BASTARD CURSES
(WRITTEN BY EARLINE MOODY)

CONTENTS
1. PREFACE
2. THE CURSE OF INCEST
    1. Scripture
    2. Incest And Bastards In The Church
    3. Comments
        1. Earline's Comments As A Teacher
3. THE CURSE OF THE BASTARD
    1. Scripture
    2. Observations About Bastards
    3. Sex Diseases And Crimes
    4. Examples
        1. Four Family Generations
        2. Unsaved To Saved
        3. The Curse Of The Bastard In Earline's Life
        4. King David
    5. Youth And Adults
        1. Young People
        2. Adults
    6. Curse Of The Bastard Bondage
    7. Abnormal Sexual Behavior In Pagan Worship
    8. Repentance And Forgiveness
4. REFERENCES

PREFACE
If anyone of your ten-generations of 2048 ancestors created a bastard or participated in incest, you are cursed. We believe that probably everyone has the curse of the bastard and the curse of incest on them, if they have not forgiven their ancestors and broken the curses off of them and their descendents.

HE CURSE OF INCEST
Scripture
Genesis 19:30-38 **Lot's two daughters committed incest with him, and conceived Moab and Ben-ammi.**
Deuteronomy 23:3-6 **One conceived in incest shall not enter into church for ten generations.**

Incest And Bastards In The Church
Incest is having sex with your blood relative, such as a father having sex with his daughter. A bastard is a child who is conceived before the parents are married.

The child is a bastard, even if the couple gets married after conception, because the sin of fornication was committed before marriage. If a child is conceived in incest, it is also a bastard. The child can have both the curses of incest and the bastard.

The child who is a bastard is cursed, its parents are cursed and ten generations of the parent's descendents are cursed. The child who has been forced into incest is cursed and its descendents are cursed for ten generations.

A bastard or incestuous person will never be content in any church, and will wander from church to church. The person will cause trouble in the churches that they attend.

Win Worley, possibly the most anointed deliverance minister in the world, loved to say "I hope you enjoyed your sin. You cursed yourself, your children, your grand children and your great-grand children."

Comments

Incest shows a degraded mind which is unclean. The person may even be filthy in his person as well as in his mind. He is degenerate in morals.

They hate those who belong to God and do every thing they can to harm them. They do not like to give aid to God's children or to God's causes. Most are critical of God's children without cause.

Rejection, bitterness and rebellion are very strong in people who have had incest relations or have this curse on them.

Children who have had incest relations will be very confused, frustrated, self accusing, hopelessly embarrassed and jealous. They will be filled with guilt, shame and evil works.

Incest causes mistrust, hatred and contempt for those in authority. They have hatred for the person who forced them into incest and often transfer that hatred to all of that sex. **This can especially lead to women hating all men.**

When they get what they feel would make them okay, it does not. They are never able to get the unwanted feelings to go away.

They are unable to accomplish anything worthwhile because their mind has become fragmented. It cannot concentrate or be disciplined.

Earline's Comments As A Teacher

It can be spotted by a teacher. These children will be scared of adults, cannot do their work alone and always are having trouble with the person in authority. They will be full of hate, bitterness, lewd talk, no self respect and no respect for others. They do not have joy in learning, do not believe things will ever change and have hopelessness with no reason to try. (The children in the first grade play with their sexual organs in the classroom.)

THE CURSE OF THE BASTARD
Scripture

Num. 22-31 The story of Balaam, Israel's idolatry, and the Midianites. Balaam was one of the God's greatest prophets but fell into sin through covetousness. Balaam advised the King of Midian to have his women mingle with the Israelites. Israel's downfall was having sex with the Midianite women and they led the men to idolatrous worship of their Gods.

Deut. 23:2 **A bastard shall not enter into church for ten generations.**

II Sam. 11:2 David conceived a bastard.

II Sam. 14-15 Household results were murder, incest and rebellion.

Rom. 1:18-32 God gave the men and women sodomites up to uncleanness through their lusts.

I Cor. 6:15-16 He which is joined to an harlot is one body; your souls are knit together.

James 3:17-18 We are looking to obtain a harvest of righteousness, not a harvest of curses.

Rev. 2:4 Because thou hast left thy first love.

Observations About Bastards

This lesson will show the far reaching effects of one act of sin by a couple. You will begin to see why our society is in such bad shape.

Here is something to consider: God has issued a three to four generation curse against the family line of those who worship other God's, but He has issued a curse for ten generations on those who conceive bastards or practice incest. God is more concerned about what we do to our offspring than about worship of other Gods.

The results of this curse fall on those conceiving the bastard, on the bastard, and an all other children born to either of them. It also falls on all of their children who are conceived inside a legitimate marriage. It falls on ten generations of descendents beginning with the bastard.

When a bastard is conceived in lust (a revelation given to Earline), it is not true love. True love is protecting and providing. Neither is present when the bastard is conceived. Demons of lust will follow all children of this line. Besides lust, other sexual demons especially will follow them and try to gain entrance.

Most babies conceived as bastards are not wanted by one or both parents. The child will have more than normal trouble with rejection, lust, anger even to commit unprovoked murder on people they do not even know, and lust even to uncontrolled lust. They will harbor hate, envy and jealousy. They will be unsettled and irresponsible. These people have a hard time sticking to a job whether it be education, profession or marriage.

They have a hard time with all intimate relationships, trouble with co-workers, sexual impurity and abnormalities, and alcohol and drugs. Fascination with crime and the occult distract from their success.

A co-operating chain of demon families work together to destroy these people in their family life, work and Christian life. These demonic families might include Ahab, Jezebel, Asmodeus, Rejection, Bitterness, Rebellion, Automatic Failure, Self-Hatred, and Excessive-Compulsive Behavior.

People with the bastard curse on them have trouble with religious deception. They cause trouble and strife in churches and groups. These demons will push people into ministry before they are grounded in Biblical principals. The intent is to destroy them before they gain sufficient strength and knowledge to stand against the attack of the demons.

These people will fall into two extremes: they will spoil for a confrontation or refuse to confront an unpleasant situation. They will dwell excessively on their problems with self or others, or they seem to be able to pretend to or ignore problems.

When they were in the womb, they were unwanted or an abortion was attempted or considered. Because of the hurt they have suffered, they become hardened and have a difficult time receiving friendship, and in giving and receiving love. They often choose a mate who will not be able to give and receive love either. They have difficulty trusting themselves or others, and often trust the wrong people thus building more hate, hurt, etc.

Present day observations of society include more bastards, family and personal rebellion, sickness, suicide, can't feel welcome or at peace in God's house, physical deformities, delinquency, murder, and mental illness.

Sex Diseases And Crimes

You should study The Bible and medical guides to see how horrible the diseases are that come out of sexual sins. It would also be shocking to study what sex crimes are, and the terrible results even unto death.

Examples
Four Family Generations

We worked with this family which included mother, daughter, grandchildren and great-grand children. Mother ran away from home at fifteen (claimed poverty was the reason), lived with a man and conceived a bastard daughter. **Mother refuses to forgive. The daughter runs away at fifteen**, lives with man, conceived a bastard granddaughter. (Do you see the pattern; like mother - like daughter.) Lives with another man, creates another bastard grandson and granddaughter. Marries, has legitimate grandson. Divorces, lives with another man and has bastard granddaughter. At present, daughter is married, found Bible, got saved and sought deliverance.

First granddaughter entices man to sex, conceives child and forces man into marriage. Second granddaughter, the step-father exposes himself to her. First grandson is very promiscuous. Second grandson is only Christian with any strength; he is very weak and unsure. Last granddaughter, thirteen years old, finds out she is also a bastard and is broken-hearted over it.

Unsaved to Saved

We went to church with this family. An unsaved drunkard conceives daughter with prostitute. Gets saved, visits daughter and finds her being raised in house of prostitution. His family agrees to take her into their home. **Curse of bastard affects even the legitimate children; one son has bastard and another son is petty criminal.**

The Curse of the Bastard in Earline's Life

Great grandfather marries great grandmother in church. All seems well; they have three children. Great grandfather dies. Great grandmother discovers she can not get his railroad pension because she is his fifth wife. My grandfather becomes very bitter and a little paranoid. My mom is paranoid and schizophrenic (like father - like daughter). She abused me physically.

Here are some of the problems created for me by this bastard curse. Never feeling at home in any church for long. Never feeling good about myself. Being ashamed for people to look at me even though I didn't know what I wanted to hide, overriding fear, striving excessively to succeed and stopping short of realizing the goal, fear of failure, fear of authority, resisting authority, fighting verbally and physically, demonic pressure to sexual activities, and not much joy in natural or spiritual life.

King David

Let's take a Bible example: David in II Sam. 11:2 conceived a bastard. The results were murder to cover it up and death to the child.

What happened to David's children as a result of this one act of disobedience? God placed a sword in David's house; it would raise up evil against David out of his own house. Nathan told David that God would have given him more wives but to take Uriah's only wife was very evil. (Notice that it was alright to have more than one wife and concubine in the Old Testament times. A concubine was a secondary wife of inferior legal status with the children being legitimate.)

David's wives would be taken by others and lain with in sight of all Israel. Household results were murder, incest and rebellion. Amnon, David's firstborn, raped his half-sister Tamar. Absalom killed Amnon in revenge; Tamar was destitute. Absalom took David's wives in the sight of Israel, and much more evil happened in David's house. In II Sam. 14-15, Absalom was very rebellious to his parents, planned to take the throne and to kill his father.

Let's look at David's first six sons: Amnon raped Tamar and then was murdered by Absalom. Of the second, Chileab, fifth, Sephatiah and sixth, Itham, no mention is made. Third, Absalom, was rebellious, murderer, attempted murder of father, and was murdered himself. Fourth, Adonijah, plotted and attempted to take David's throne when David had his last illness. **These sons had total disregard for God's house.**

(Do you have a sword hanging over your family of adultery, murder, abortion, incest, bastard or other sexual sins?)

Youth And Adults
Young People
If things severely pressure you. If you have tendency to perversions or violence, agitating passion, moral conflict, and craving or covetousness, perhaps the bastard curse is on you. Does crime fascinate you, are you excessively self conscious, are you ashamed for people to look at you even when you don't know why, have an unusual desire to please peers and adults, fear of not being accepted by God, sell yourself for nothing, don't respect yourself, don't trust and obey God or parents, deviate from God's moral code, and have no joy and are double-minded?

Where does true joy come from? Only a clear pure heart can have true joy. This joy abides through trouble. All other joy is either partial or counterfeit.

Adults
If you have the same problems as the young people, including the inability to love, guide and lead your children into a Godly life, you also may have the bastard's curse or you may have started it.

Curse Of The Bastard Bondage
Each time a bastard is created, whether it comes to birth or is aborted, ten generations of bondage is started. **Ten generations of ancestors is 2048 people that can affect you in ten-generation curse.** When you and your mate conceive a bastard, there is no way to calculate how many people will be affected. **An example is the Jukes Family which affected 1200 people in six generations.**

Abnormal Sexual Behavior In Pagan Worship
Earline learned to research demonic names and practices. This exposes a lot of what is wrong with Christian traditions. Read and study these scriptures: Num. 22-31, Rom. 1:18-32, Rev. 2:4, and I Cor. 6:15-16. See Strong's Concordance (everyone should have a copy) under **Ashtoreth, Ashtaroth, Queen of Heaven, and Tammuz**. If you look these names up in Biblical dictionaries and encyclopedias, as well as secular dictionaries and encyclopedias, you will see that all forms of **deviate and demonic sexual behavior** is the basis of their worship. **As we engage in these sexual acts, we are worshiping Satan (Earline's revelation). Whether we realize we are worshiping Satan or not does not make any difference in the consequences.** As it is very difficult for people to leave their religions, so it is hard for people to give up immoral sex acts once they have engaged in them.

Repentance And Forgiveness
Repentance and forgiveness are absolute necessities. We must see this sin as God sees it. For worshipping other Gods (idols), only three to four generations are cursed; but for conceiving a bastard - ten generations. A Bible generation is forty years; this curse runs

400 years if no one repeats it after the first occurrence. Next, we must break the curse of the bastard and call out the demons. After this is done, we must renew and discipline our mind and body.

Jesus became accursed for us. We have the privilege of breaking this curse, obtaining our family's freedom and living Godly lives that will not profane God before the heathen. We are looking to obtain a harvest of righteousness in James 3:17-18, not a harvest of curses.

REFERENCES
Deliverance Manual by Gene and Earline Moody

SECTION 13 - BREAKING THE CURSE OFF BLACK AMERICA

The African-American race labors under tremendous curses and afflictions. This race of people all behave the same. Many were high on crack cocaine, drunk on alcohol, unwed teenage mothers walking around with babies in their arms, young people driving expensive cars obtained largely from drug sale profits, ladies purposely dressed seductively, young men exposing their underwear, a staggering number of African-American male population filling the prisons, embracing homosexuality, prostitution and all sorts of perversion.

The result of disobedience is death. God's reward for sin, iniquities, perversions, and those who walk contrary to His Word is death - natural and spiritual.

There are various types of perversions: spiritual, sexual, financial, etc. Financial perversion encompasses - but is not limited to - cheating, stealing, robbery, bribes, covetousness, deceit, gambling, and unlawful gain. Perverse speech denotes lying, slander, cursing and swearing, and speaking blasphemous words.

African-Americans are a people group (ethnic) born of the seed of slavery. The mixture of races of Africans, Europeans, and Indians has produced a mixed breed now called African-American. Black America is under a curse of plagues, and vexations resulting in calamities - instead of blessings - overtaking them. Blessings and curses rests upon families, communities, and even entire nations.

An apparent consequence of the history of enslavement, bondage, and oppression is two fold: the belief of many Black Americans that they will never be free; and the opportunity that this belief provides for Satan to establish stronghold over this people group.

Among legally married persons, regardless of geographic region in the U.S., blacks are at greatest risk. Young black males are dying untimely deaths - it's a war zone of mass destruction. It is a perpetuated cycle of poverty and crime in the black community.

Forty million babies have been killed by abortion since 1973 when abortion was legalized, and 14 million of them were black. The aim of the program was to restrict - many believe exterminate - the black population with the Negro Project.

Black leaders must teach the truth from their pulpits, live the truth daily, and avoid making excuses for their insufficiencies. Therefore, some of the conditions under which many of the people exist are the primary responsibility of black church leaders.

The prevalence of high blood pressure in blacks in the United States is among the highest in the world. Blacks have almost twice the risk of first-ever strokes compared with whites. Among the leading cancers, prostate cancer among black men is about 15 times higher than among white men and 2.7 times higher than among Asian/Pacific Islander men.

In studies that compare individuals with similar levels of income and education, blacks have a shorter life expectancy than any other racial group. The Census Bureau indicated that by 2010 there would be only 85 black men for every 100 black women.

The lack of parental involvement has caused low self-esteem, lack of motivation to learn, laziness, apathy, and a lack of accountability among too many of the young people. Growing up uncovered, unprotected, unnourished, without a father, abandonment, total rejection, generational curses, and emptiness left by the absence of father.

Approximately 25 per 1,000 black children were confirmed victims of maltreatment, more than double the national average and the highest victimization rate among racial groups represented.

HIV was the number one cause of death for blacks between the ages of 25 and 44 in 2000. In 2002, the leading cause of HIV infection among black men was sexual contact with other men (sodomy or homosexual activity), followed by injection drug use and heterosexual contact. In 2002, blacks have the highest STD rates in the nation. Of new infections among men in the United States, approximately 60% of men were infected through homosexual sex, 25% through injection drug use, and 15% through heterosexual sex.

If the sin was sexual, it could bring adultery, incest, children from incestuous union, children born out-of-wedlock, destroy virginity, bestiality, homosexuality, lesbianism, and sodomy. Other curses come from parents, pastors, rulers, and authorities turning away from God, idolatry, pride, fleshly practices, and touching or harming God's anointed.

There are very few members living according to biblical principles, including the pastor and deacons. In reality, man-made traditions, man-made customs, and simply put, the flesh, are the guiding factors of the church. Sin is rampant with God appearing to be powerless to stop it. The lack of integrity of the ministerial leadership, the strongholds, bondages, and traditions of the Black Church. The profaneness has been released upon Black America by the spiritual leaders. Black America has paid a dear price for ignorance. The immoral activities and sensual behavior patterns have cost families and in some case lives.

The civil rights era was a turning point for Black America. After many protests, beatings, persecution, and marches, blacks began to be recognized as a people group. Rev. King's sexual escapades were intertwined with his manhood, just like other men of the cloth who were preoccupied or infatuated with love. We can determine that after Rev. Martin L. King, Jr. died, the symptoms of the curse broke forth and continued to multiply even until today. SCLC was a rowdy group that engaged in partying, featuring prostitution and even sexual harassment. There was a great release of spiritual profaneness by black leaders that has continued unto this day.

If church leaders are living in sin, what can be expected from Black America? There is no need to cover-up and shift the blame to others for the dilemma and continue to play the victim.

Christians are just churching and sin is running rampant in the church, especially among today's leaders. Don't do as I do, do as I say is the principle. For years, deceit, mistrust, and lack of spiritual discipline and truth have eaten away at the core of these once hallowed organizations.

Today, more than ever before, men of the cloth are fornicating, and having children by women within their congregations. Sexual immoralities and perversion abide more inside the church than outside the church. All they can see is fame and fortune, but few look deep into the hurts, fears, and weaknesses of those who give the appearance that all is well.

We are beholding the fruit of sin, and it seems that whatever we wanted to happen is operating in reverse. Judges have been led away in handcuffs, and some black judges have been disbarred. A dark cloud appears to hover over Black America and the people are engulfed in a culture of sin. The Democratic Party is consistently on the wrong side of moral issues. That party led the way for abortion and homosexuality legislation. A culture of sin has fallen upon the black community, and it is in denial and refuses to hear the truth. Immorality is running rampant, touching every sector of the black community, starting with the leaders.

Many churches are in need of help, not having good leadership. There are pastors who cannot be found. There are ladies in churches who are laboring, even when men cannot be found and leadership is lacking.

Be assured, no matter how small the sin, it will be exposed when God reveals it in His own time. Many pastors and leaders are fully aware of the sins and demonic strongholds with which they are living. Many pastors are living a lie. Their man concern is for wealth and status.

Spiritual darkness is encountered everywhere. Some well-known preachers are living a lie. Many leaders in the Black Church are stumbling repeatedly as though the Lord cannot direct their path. There are bad batches of worship and praises going up to God in the black churches.

Much of the work of the Black Church is acceptable to man, but not unto God as it is done grudgingly and of necessity. There is a dire need for black leaders to see clearly in the Spirit. There is too much immorality in the Black Church, namely greed, pedophilia, homosexuality, lesbianism, adultery, and fornication. Immorality, unethical practices, and evil have spread in the church.

Homosexuals are directing church choirs and some are pastors and members of the clergy. There are many homosexuals taking over the music ministries (pastors are being held hostage).

The poverty and slavery mentality needs to be transformed, and strongholds of hopelessness and despair destroyed. Self-hatred and hatred for others needs to diminish. Black America needs to humble itself, and confess and repent for its sins and shortcomings on a national basis.

Sexually wounded and scarred females and males need to be healed. They have been victims to mental and physical illnesses, witness protection programs, drug rehabilitation centers, and welfare institutions. If God's call is not heeded and His cure not responded to, the curses will worsen.

REFERENCE
Breaking the Curse off Black America by Willie F. Wooten, Lumen-us Publications, Richton Park, IL

SECTION 14 - CURSE OF AHAB AND JEZEBEL
(Written By Earline Moody)

CONTENTS
1. LIST OF SCRIPTURE ABOUT AHAB, JEZEBEL AND OTHERS
    1. Scripture
    2. Other Families In The Bible
    3. Ahab
    4. Jezebel
2. CURSES FOUND IN THE BIBLE
3. TESTIMONIES ABOUT AHAB AND JEZEBEL
4. AHAB/JEZEBEL
5. RESULTS OF AHAB/JEZEBEL RELATIONSHIP
6. AHAB/JEZEBEL REBELLIOUS INFLUENCE IN THE WORLD
7. EFFECT ON CHILDREN OF AHAB/JEZEBEL
8. YOU AND PEOPLE AROUND YOU
9. CURSE OF AHAB - SCRIPTURE EXPLANATION
10. AHAB CHARACTERISTICS
11. GENE'S AHAB CHARACTERISTICS
13. AHAB REBELS
14. JEZEBEL REBELS
15. ELIJAH DESTROYS BAAL'S PROPHETS
16. PRAYER
17. AHAB AND JEZEBEL DEMONS (Short List)
    1. Ahab Demons
    2. Jezebel Demons
18. AHAB AND JEZEBEL DEMONS (Long List)
    1. Ahab Demons
    2. Jezebel Demons
19. REFERENCES

LIST OF SCRIPTURE ABOUT AHAB, JEZEBEL AND OTHERS
Scripture

Matt. 12:43-45 <u>Empty</u>, swepth and garnished (<u>unoccupied</u>, swepth, put in order and decorated).
John 8:44 Ye are of your father, the Devil.

Other Families In The Bible
Learn to identify mistakes the people made as you read their stories. The only person that didn't make any mistakes was THE LORD JESUS CHRIST!

Gen.3   (Eve) Jezebel Spirit.
    3:3   (Eve) Added to GOD's Words.
    3:6   (Eve) Did wrong and persuaded Adam too.
    16:1   (Sarah) Act of Jezebel.

	16:5	**(Sarah & Hagar) Contention and strife - results of Jezebel.**
	21:9	**(Isaac & Ishmael) Forever strife of nations.**
	25:23	**(Rebekah) Knew Jacob was to rule over Esau.**
	25:29	**(Jacob) Also has Jezebel spirit. Connives to get birthright; results in confusion**
	27:1-29	(Rebekah & Jacob) Again connives to get blessing.
	27:41	**(Esau) Hates Jacob.**
	27:46	**(Rebekah & Jacob) Fear.**
	25 & 27	(Report of contention, strife & wearing down of families)

Read Isaiah 3:12 (Children and women rule). Is this the situation in your home? If so, it is out of divine order.

Ahab

I Kings	16:**25, 28, 30-33,** 39
	17:1
	18:1, **4, 13, 17-19, 21, 24-26, 28-29,** 46
	19:**1-3,** 42
	20:2, 13-14, 34, 42-43
	21:1, **3-5,** 7, **15-16, 18-21, 24-25,** 27, **29**
	22:1, 3-4, 6, **8-9,** 20, **27,** 30, 34, 38-41, 49-50, 52
II Kings	1:1-2, 17
	3:**1-2,** 5
	8:16, **18,** 25, 27-29
	9:**7-10, 22,** 25, **29-37**
	10:1, 10-11, 17-18, 30
	21:3, 13, 23
II Chronicles	18:**1-3,** 19
	21:6, 13
	22:3-8
Jeremiah	29:21-22
Micah	6:16
Revelation	2:20

Jezebel

I Kings	16:31
	18:4, 13, 19, **17-40**
	19:1-2
	21:5, **25**
II Kings	9:7, 37
Revelation	2:30

CURSES FOUND IN THE BIBLE

Men may also have Jezebelic tendencies; women - Abab tendencies. The relationship of Ahab and Jezebel provides an excellent illustration of the curse brought about by a husband and wife being out of GOD's divine order for the family.

This curse can be traced back all the way to Adam and Eve. It can be found through the Bible being manifested in different families.

GOD puts the greatest burden of responsibility on the men, not the women. If the men were not Ahabs and were, in fact, priests and heads of their homes, then the women would not be Jezebels! **The Ahab man cannot escape his responsibility by blaming his problems on the Jezebelic woman.**

TESTIMONIES ABOUT AHAB AND JEZEBEL
The Bible provides a lot of stories about families with Ahab / Jezebel tendencies. It is very interesting to trace the sins of the ancestors down through the generations in the Bible. Not only can you see the sins passed down through the men but also through the women.

AHAB / JEZEBEL
Do you have more than the usual problems in finance, housing, family, etc.? This may be the curse of improper family structure. If someone does not stop the pattern of living in the curse, it will go from generation to generation.

A mother who is a Jezebel will raise Jezebel daughters and Ahab sons. Ahab fathers will raise Ahab sons and Jezebel daughters. If sons do not see their father as respected in his office of father, they have no other example to the contrary and will follow him. Likewise, the girls will probably choose a husband like their father. Do you see this happening?

When you have a Jezebel / Ahab marriage, you will have men not committed to GOD, home or children. These men prefer to play and pretend they are men, and only deceive themselves. Likewise, the women who have to take over the financial care and sometimes total responsibility for the children are equally deceived.

RESULTS OF AHAB / JEZEBEL RELATIONSHIP
1. We set the wrong pattern for our children to follow.
2. The children spend the rest of their adult lives trying to live normal lives.
3. Husbands are wrongly influenced by their wives.
4. Husbands let the wives do their jobs.
5. Ahab men are weak spiritually and may be evil.
6. Ahab men turn away from their families and GOD to achieve satisfaction in other things such as wine, women and money.
7. We shift our blame to the other party.
8. The women are placed in a position of priest and head of the home which they cannot handle.
9. We open our families, churches and nation to demonic attack.

AHAB / JEZEBEL REBELLIOUS INFLUENCE IN THE WORLD
1. Divorce - one parent families.
2. Felinism - pictures bungling father and clever mother.

3. Sex - no restrictions.
4. Young people - confused, rebellious.
5. Drugs - Sex - Music.
6. Society with emotional problems.
7. Effeminate, emotional, weak spiritual and physical men.
8. Women's false strength put to test usually fails.

EFFECT ON CHILDREN OF AHAB / JEZEBEL

Children are open to violence or death, even early death, because of tensions, confusions, hurts and insults given them by the family structure being out of order **(Eze. 38:8-9)**. Confusion, frustration, disgust, hate, etc. lead to suicide. In trying to find their place, these children frequently give in to spirits which drive them to love of power, money, praise, fame, etc. (I Kings 21:20).

Children have fear, insecurity, frustration and difficulty learning. It leads to potential corruption, discord, growth in occult and cults, selfishness, doubt, inability to achieve, fake sickness, hypochondriacs and church splits.

Ahab fathers place curses on male children; Jezebel mothers -female children. Male children tend to become homosexuals; female children - lesbians. Children will have broken marriages and families like their parents. Jezebel mothers cause children to be manipulative. Children are full of rebellion and under pressure to prove their love to their parents. **Finally, children are open to satanic attack and will usually become like their parents!**

YOU AND PEOPLE AROUND YOU

Such qualities as these have **unnatural power to seduce you,** even overwhelm you. It is not charisma but seduction, and it creates bondage. You may have a friend whom you at times have a great desire to be free of, and the next moment feel guilt or condemnation for desiring your freedom. Consider why you are attracted to your friend.

Look out for moms and dads who try to dominate married children's lives, and men and women who **cannot delegate authority** but try to mind every detail.

Women and men shouldn't try to force mate into a religious experience, but win him or her by quiet and joyful submission to the Christian life, **fulfilling your role as GOD established it.**

CURSE OF AHAB - SCRIPTURE EXPLANATION

Omri was an idol (demon) worshipper and Ahab's father; Omri did worse than all the kings before him. He set the pattern for his son to follow and Ahab did evil in the sight of THE LORD above all that were before him, even Omri (I Kings 16:25, 28 & 30).

He married Jezebel, daughter of Ethbaal, king of the Zidonians who worshipped Baal. So Ahab served and worshipped Baal. Ahab was influenced spiritually by Jezebel. Baal was the male God; Asherah - female God (I Kings 16:31;18:17-19).

Ahab told Elijah that he, not Ahab, was the one that troubled Israel. Ahab would not take his responsibility but shifted blame for his problems and those of his father (I Kings 18:21). He persecuted the prophets (I Kings 18:4, 13 & 19).

Ahab told Jezebel about Elijah killing the prophets of Baal. Jezebel was the one that took action against Elijah (vowed to kill him), not Ahab. He let her do his job (I Kings 19:1).

Ahab not only worshipped Baal; he was disobedient to GOD and did not follow Elijah's prophecies.

He grieved over not getting Naboth's vineyard; he was greedy. Ahab let Jezebel do his dirty work of stealing the vineyard. Then he did not mind about hearing of Naboth's death. He sold himself to Satan to work evil (I Kings 21:4. 7, 16, 19-20).

His children were affected by the deeds of Ahab (I Kings 21:21).

He was dominated by his wife to do evil. GOD forgave him when he humbled himself before GOD (I Kings 21:25 & 29).

He hated the truth and the prophets of GOD. He was willing to imprison and torture them (I Kings 22:8 & 27).

He was subtle and willing to use Jehoshaphat as a decoy to be attacked.

Ahab's son was Ahaziah; he followed his parents' evil ways. He followed Baalzebub, the God of Eberon.

Another son of Ahab, Joram, did evil but not like his parents (II Kings 3:1-2).

Jehoram married the daughter of Ahab; he also did evil in THE LORD's sight. He was crafty like Ahab (II Kings 8:18, II Chron. 18:2). He also persecuted the prophets (II Kings 9:7 & 22).

The death of Jezebel is foretold and happens as predicted (II Kings 9:10 & 30-37).

AHAB CHARACTERISTICS

He brought grief and judgement on himself and the nation. He opened the floodgates for idol worship into the nation. He did not oppose murder for greed or any other purpose. Once entered into the mind of an Ahab man, he will accept more and more wanton acts of a depraved nature. There is a loss of manhood and fatherhood.

Jezebel's aim was accurate in spiritual perspective, but her acts were against GOD and His plan. So, by not opposing Jezebel, Ahab gave consent and is guilty of being an accessory to the crime.

Satan's evil desires are seen in the evil acts of men (John 8:44). Influence is what a demon does to you from the outside; control - inside. You have to be careful what you allow to influence you because demons hope to gain control later on through that influence.

Ahab broke the Ten Commandments; he coveted the man's field.

Ahab married a woman devoted to everything that GOD hated and forbid. This opened a breach upon Israel through which Satan gained astonishing power and flooded Israel with evil. Even so, a man opposed to GOD who submits to his wife or other women, opens the floodgate for evil to pour upon his family.

GENE'S AHAB CHARACTERISTICS
1. Leaving spiritual leadership up to Earline about how to raise children.
2. Breakdown of communications between Earline, Marie and me as I pursued spiritual goals but neglected my family.
3. Fear of getting hurt by others especially by my family and Earline's family.
4. God of jobs at one time when I put my job first, family second and GOD last. Now it is reversed: **GOD first, family second and job last.**
5. Leaving things of GOD to wife occurred partially such as receiving the Baptism Of The Holy Spirit. I suggested that Earline receive it first.
6. I came from a poor family and had a materialistic drive until Byron died.
7. We had many misunderstandings as Ahab husband and Jezebel wife.
8. I did not believe in having an argument with my wife. So, I would go into my room, study engineering, and not talk to Earline.
9. We even came close to separation and divorce at our low point years ago after Byron died.
10. I was somewhat unemotional and could not show love the way I should.
11. The greatest blessing was that GOD kept us from whole-heartedly pursuing fame and fortune before Byron died.
12. Earline said I acted like an Ahab but did not give in anytime!

AHAB REBELS
The major rebellion was against GOD in Baal worship. He went after other idols. Worshipping idols is the worst rebellion against GOD.

Ahab exhibited characteristics of confusion, disobedience, resentfulness, sullenness and greed. He was an accomplice to Jezebel, believed a lying spirit, refused to believe GOD, and begat rebellious children.

JEZEBEL REBELS
She killed GOD's prophets which is **rebellion against GOD.** She exhibited hate, retaliation and threatenings.

She turns from the role of woman and wife to trying to upstage the King, her husband. She belittled him, connived behind his back, and plotted murder and control of people.

Some women and men today use seemingly pure religious motives to control others such as prophecy - telling others what to do (soulish prophecy is charismatic witchcraft).

Another motive behind her rebellion was that she **wanted worship and admiration.**

Jezebelic actions are true sorcery. Rebellious Jezebelic males / females will ask questions aimed at causing the other person to doubt their worth, ability, decisions, etc.

She ended up being thrown out a window, run over by chariots and eaten by dogs. **She probably went to Hell.**

ELIJAH DESTROYS BAAL'S PROPHETS (I KINGS 18:17-40)

If you believe that JESUS IS LORD, He said to cast out demons (envoys of Satan) and He said don't cast them out of the unsaved (Matt. 12:43-45 & I Kings 18:21).

Many times in deliverance sessions, the demons inside someone will cry out for help. If the demon power is bound in JESUS' Name, the demon gets no help. The Name of JESUS answers by actions and the demon leaves. Who is greater: JESUS or Satan (I Kings 18:24)?

GOD's people should dictate directions and conditions, not Satan (I Kings 18:25).

It is tough on Satan when he is on open display; he does not like talk of demons. As long as he is hidden, he has power; but shown in the light of GOD, he limps around (I Kings 18:26).

Satanist cut themselves, eat flesh and drink blood (I Kings 18:28).

The Devil usually will not exhibit himself when GOD's presence is real but will manifest when people give their will over to his direction. **The devil made me do it** is always a lie! (I Kings 18:29).

PRAYER

I ask you to forgive me and I forgive my ancestors for being Jezebels and Ahabs. Please forgive me for idol worship, passivity, irresponsibility, fear, weakness, sexual impurity, pride, selfishness, witchcraft, control, criticism, jealousy, rebellion, competition, retaliation, marriage breaking, child abuse and worshiping other Gods. I ask this in THE NAME OF JESUS CHRIST: LORD, MASTER AND SAVIOR. I command the spirits to manifest, identify and reveal themselves. I command the families of demons to come out as your name is called.

AHAB AND JEZEBEL DEMONS
(Short List)

Ahab Demons

Ahab	Idol Worship
Abdicating Leadership	Impotence
Adultery	Joblessness
Aggression	Laziness
Angry	
Bitterness	Lust
Communication breakdown	Lust of material things
Conditional love	Lack of confidence
Childish behavior	Liking sensual women
Competition	Macho spirit
Covetousness	Misunderstandings
Compromise	Manipulating women
Clashing conflict	Murder
Considering GOD's things trivial	No order
Call evil good - good, evil	No peace
Displeased	No unity
Disobedient	Overloading wife
Dirty stories	Pride
Degradation	Pornography
Destruction of family priesthood	Pouting
Doubting manhood	Passive quitter
Drunkenness	Rebellious children
Emasculations	Rejection
Emotional cripple	Resentment
Failure	Scared
Fearful	Separation & divorce
Fear of getting hurt	Sibling rivalry
Fear of women	Sluggishness
Filth	Stoicism
Following sins of the father	Tragic mistakes
God of sports	Unemotional
God of jobs	Upset children
Heavy spirited	Workaholic
Hatred of women	
Homosexuality	
Hurts	

Inability to designate authority
Leaving things of GOD to wife
Worship of enterprise, success, profit, promotion & wealth

Jezebel Demons

- Accusation
- Aggression
- Attention seeking
- Arrogance
- Beguiling
- Belittling
- Bickering
- Backbiting
- Brash, bossy woman
- Bedroom blackmail
- Conniving
- Contention
- Continuous complaining
- Condemnation
- Confusion
- Counterfeit spiritual gifts
- Conditional love
- Charming
- Controlling spirits
- Dissatisfaction
- Demands
- Double Mindedness
- Doubt
- Disunity
- Discord
- Disruption
- Distrust
- Deception
- Delusion
- Demanding
- Defeat
- Determined maneuvers
- Dominance
- Emotional outburst
- Failure
- Fear
- Frustration
- Forsaking protection
- Female dominance & control
- Female hardness
- Fierce determination
- False sickness
- Finger pointing
- Frigidity
- Indecision
- Intimidation
- Insinuation
- Insecurity
- Inadequate
- Intellectualism
- Inhospitable
- Interference
- Jealousy
- Jezebel
- Lack of confidence
- Lying
- Lawlessness
- Laziness
- Manipulation
- Mistrust
- Nagging
- Overindulgence
- Pouting
- Pride
- Psychology
- Philosophy
- Projected guilt
- Quick temper
- Retaliation
- Revenger
- Rationalization
- Rebellion
- Strife
- Slander
- Sharp temper
- Short temper
- Sorcery
- Sensitive
- Sharp tongue
- Sleepiness
- Shame
- Suicide
- Spiritual blindness
- Self-defeating
- Sorrow
- Turmoil

Grief
Hatred of men
Hot temper
Hasty marriage
Hopelessness
Hypnotic control
Inability to give or receive love
Irresponsibility

Ungodly discipline
Unbelief
Ugliness
Vanity
Whining
Witchcraft
Worldly wisdom

Perversion (sexual & spiritual)
Shirking responsibilities

AHAB AND JEZEBEL DEMONS
(Long List)
(Jezebel And The Goddesses - How You Can Defeat Them)

Ahab Demons

Son Of Jezebel
Son Of Ahab
Father of Jezebel
Father of Ahab

Passivity
Laziness
Inertia
Lethargy
Sloth
Indolent
Inactivity
Avoiding Work
"I Hate Working"
Don't Want To Work

Irresponsibility
Unreliability
Childishness
Pouting
Temper Tantrums
Lassitude
Undependability
Carelessness
Ineptitude
Foolishness
Little Boy
Mama's Boy
Good Old Boy

Fear
Of Responsibility
Of Authority
Of Rebuke
Of Ridicule
Of Failing
Blaming Wife
Blaming Others

Weakness
 Insecurity
Indecision
Compromise
Lack Of Character
Lack Of Authority
Leaning On Wife
Leaning On Others
Milque-Toast

Sexual Impurity
Impotence
Homosexuality
Effeminate
Succubus

124

Emasculation

(For additional demons, see Jezebel list.)

Names Of The Gods
Baal
Baalim
Bel
Belial
Perseus
Phoroneus
Nimrod
Nin
Tammuz
Lord Of Heaven
The Sun
Belus
Merodach
Osiris
Horus
Apis
Saurun
Baal-Berith
Baal-Zebub
Baal-Sutekh
El-Berith
Lord Of The Flies
Kronos
"Bread Of Life"
Nin
Ninus
Dyonisius
Bacchus
Iacchus
Siva, Shiva
Moloch

Ahab: If you have cast out the previous demons, cast Ahab out now.)

(Note: The names of **Sexual Impurity** demons are essentially the same for Jezebel and Ahab with the exception of female or male demons.)

Jezebel Demons

Daughter of Jezebel
Daughter of Ahab
Mother of Jezebel
Mother of Ahab

Sexual Impurity
Lust
Fantasy Lust
Defilement
Adultery
Fornication
Incest
Exposure
Frigidity
Smut
Filth
Oral Sex
Anal Sex
Sodomy
Take Me
Rape
Obscenity
Pornography
Child Pornography
Child Molestation
Pornographic Flashbacks
Pornographic Memory
Burning Passion
Harlotry
Prostitution
Sexual Incitement
Sexual Enticement
Lesbianism
Homosexuality
Bi-Sexual
Cross Dresser
Transvestite
Exhibitionism
Flirting

Pride
Haughtiness
Ego
Self
Egotism
Conceit
Vanity
Self-Righteousness
Self-Importance, "The Queen"
Arrogance
Center of Attention
Superiority
Pride of Life
Self-Sufficiency
Pretension

Selfishness
Egoism
Egotism
Egocentric
Egomania
Number One
Self-Centered
Self-Obsessed
Self-Idolatry
Self-Admiration
Self-Approval
Self-Interest
Self-Concern
Self-Seeker
Taker, not Giver
People User
Inconsiderate
Narcissistic

Lust of the Eyes
Lust of the Flesh
Inordinate Affection
Nymphomania
Masturbation
Sadism
Masochism
Dominatrix
Satyrism
Seduction
Sensuality
  Incubus
Perversity
Perverse Spirit
Cupid
Eros

Witchcraft
Charismatic Witchcraft
White Magic
Black Magic
Sorcery
Fortune Telling
Horoscopes
Astrology
Tarot Cards
Crystal Ball
ESP
Mind Control
Conjurations
Incantations
Potions
Burning Of Dedicated Candles
Channeling
Crystals
Wicca
Satanism
Charms
Fetishes
Levitation
Palmistry
Handwriting Analysis
Hair Reading
Iridiology
Automatic Handwriting
Ouija Board

Abortion
Child Abuse
Child Neglect
Child Abandonment
Child Murderer

Control
Possessiveness
Dominance
Deception
Ascendancy
Lying
Manipulation
Scheming
Strategy
String-Pulling
Wire-Pulling
Do It My Way
Authoritarian
Tyrannical
Argumentative
Upper Hand
Whip Hand
Ruler
Master
Revenge

Criticism
Critical Spirit
Judgmental, Judging
Accusation
Fault-Finding
Censure
Prejudice

Jealousy
Envy
Suspicion
Distrust
Covetousness
Greed
Discontent

Rebellion
Willfulness
Disobedience

Pendulum
Divination
Enchantment
Fire Gazing
Astral Projection
Kabala
Hypnosis
Medium
Psychic Powers
Psychokinesis
Telepathy
Table Tipping
Talismans
Fetishes
Santeria
Voodoo
"The Witch"
Poltergeist
Tea Leaf Reading
Palmistry
Curses
Hexes
Vexes

Retaliation
Destruction
Spite
Hatred
Malice
Treachery

Marriage-Breaking
Hatred Of Husband
Despising Husband
Belittling
Lack Of Intimacy
Arguing
Contentious
Anti-Submissiveness
Distance
Separation
Divorce
Asmodeus
Osmodeus
Matrimonial Discord
Never Satisfied

Anti-Submissiveness
Stubbornness
Defiance
Opposition
Resistance
Obstinacy

Competition
I'm Better Than You
I Am The Best
I Win
What I Think Is The Way It Is
What I Say Is The Way It Is
I Have The Last Word
I Am More Important
My Choices Are The Best
I Go In First
I Know Better
Competitive
Arguing
Driving
Pride
Ego
Headstrong
Intimidating
Strife
Contention
Disagreement
Debate
Altercation
Quarreling
Discussion
Controvert
Conflict
Dissension
Friction
Fighting
Battle
Clash
Combat
Dispute
Assert
Maintain
Insist

Child Abuse
Provocation
Disrespect Of Sons (or Daughters)
Belittlement Of Sons (or Daughters)
Humiliation Of Sons (or Daughters)
Hatred Of Sons (or Daughters)
Jealousy Of Sons (or Daughters)
Negligence Of Sons (or Daughters)
Destruction Of Sons (or Daughters)
Physical Abuse
Mental Abuse
Emotional Abuse
Psychological Abuse
Verbal Abuse
Sexual Abuse
Incest Abortion
Murder
Moloch

Goddesses Of The Feminist Movement
Songi
Athena
Tara
Pasowee
Ishtar
Ixmucane
Adita
Nashe

Wiccan Goddesses
Artemis
Astarte
Athene
Dione
Melusine
Aphrodite
Cerridwen
Dana
Arianhod
Isis
Bride
Changing Woman
Shakti

Names of Goddesses
Ashera
Asherim
Ashtaroth

Ashtoreth
Athirat
Astarte
Astoreth Of The Sidonians
Ishtar
Goddess Of The Groves
Athirat
Asterie
Astrea
Themis
Virgin Themis
The Perfect One
Goddess Of Justice
Semiramis
Beltis
Queen Of Heaven
Eve
Aphrodite
Mylitta
The Mediatrix
Woman Mediator
Melitza
Melissa
Rhea
Cybele
Melitta
Venus
Archia
Arkh
Diana
Diana Of The Ephesians
Diana Of The Romans
Artemis
Moon Goddess
Ash-Toret

Semiramis
Immaculately Conceived
Blessed Virgin Mary
Aida Odeo
Beltis
Goddess Of Wisdom
Anahita
Ardvi Sura Anahita
Anat
Anath
Atargatis
Isis
Ceres
Shing-Moo
Sati
Virgin Mary
Re-Anen
Josephine
Delilah
St. Barbara
Aida-Odeo
Mother Of The Gods
Mother Of Lies
Mother Of Cheating
Inanna
Enheduanna
Gaia
Hather
Demeter
Kali
Ariadne

Ash-Turit
Mother Of The Gods
Minerva
Athena

Jezebel: If you have cast out all the previous demons, cast out Jezebel now.)

(Note: although Delilah, Eve and Josephine are not Goddesses, they have been added because they are found as demons among the demons of the Goddesses. I believe Josephine refers to the wife of Napoleon.)

REFERENCES
Jezebel And The Goddesses - How You Can Defeat Them, by Mitsi Burton, Impact Christian Books, Kirkwood, MO

SECTION 15 - CURSES OF THE SERPENT

CONTENTS
1. TREAD ON SERPENTS
2. CORRUPTING BEGUILING SUBTLE SERPENT
3. FIERY SERPENT WORSHIP
4. SERPENT TONGUES
5. SERPENT BITES
6. PIERCING CROOKED DRAGON SERPENT
7. DRAGON DEVIL SATAN SERPENT
8. COMMENTS

TREAD ON SERPENTS
Luke 10:19 Behold, I give unto you power (delegated authority) to tread on serpents and scorpions (demonic angels and spirits) and over all the power of the enemy (the kingdom of evil) and nothing shall by any means hurt you. (power - tread - nothing).

CORRUPTING BEGUILING SUBTLE SERPENT
Gen. 3:1 Now the serpent was more subtil (crafty) than any beast of the field which THE LORD GOD had made. And he said unto the woman, Yea, hath GOD said, Ye shall not eat of every tree of the garden?
Gen. 3:2 And the woman said unto the serpent, We may eat of the fruit of the trees of the garden:
Gen. 3:4 And the serpent said unto the woman. Ye shall not surely die:
Gen. 3:13 And THE LORD GOD said unto the woman, What is this that thou hast done? And the woman said, The serpent beguiled (cheated, outwitted and deceived) me, and I did eat.
Gen. 3:14 And THE LORD GOD said unto the serpent, Because thou hast done this, thou art cursed above all cattle, and above every beast of the field, upon thy belly shalt thou go, and dust shalt thou eat all the days of thy life:
2 Cor. 11:3 But I fear, lest by any means, as the serpent beguiled (cunning) Eve through his subtilty, so your minds should be corrupted (seduced) from the simplicity that is in CHRIST.

FIERY SERPENT WORSHIP
Num. 21:8 And THE LORD said unto Moses, Make thee a fiery serpent, and set it upon a pole: and it shall come to pass, that every one that is bitten, when he looketh upon it, shall live.
Num. 21:9 And Moses made a serpent of brass, and put it upon a pole, and it came to pass, that if a serpent had bitten any man, when he beheld the serpent of brass, he lived.
2 Kings 18:4 He removed the high places, and brake the images, and cut down the groves, and brake in pieces the brazen serpent that Moses had made: for unto those days the children of Israel did burn incense to it: and he called it Nehushtan.
John 3:14 And as Moses lifted up the serpent in the wilderness, even so must the Son Of Man be lifted up:

SERPENT TONGUES
Psa. 140:3 They have sharpened their tongues like a serpent; adder's poison is under their lips. Selah.

SERPENT BITES
Ecc. 10:11 Surely the serpent will bite without enchantment (charming); and a babbler (slanderer) is no better.

PIERCING CROOKED DRAGON SERPENT
Isa. 27:1 In that day THE LORD with his sore and great and strong sword shall punish leviathan the piercing serpent, even leviathan the crooked serpent; and he shall slay the dragon that is in the sea.

DRAGON DEVIL SATAN SERPENT
Rev. 12:9 And the great dragon was cast out, that old serpent, called the Devil, and Satan, which deceiveth the whole world: he was cast out into the earth, and his angels were cast out with him.
Rev. 12:15 And the serpent cast out of his mouth water as a flood after the woman, that he might cause her to be carried away of the flood.
Rev. 20:2 And he laid hold on the dragon, that old serpent, which is the Devil, and Satan, and bound him a thousand years.

COMMENTS
We have power to tread on serpents and scorpions (Demonic Angels and Spirits) and over all the power of the enemy (The Kingdom Of Evil) and nothing shall by any means hurt you. (Power - Tread - Nothing). **We have Delegated Authority over Demonic Angels and Spirits, and over The Kingdom Of Evil which includes Satan, fallen angels and demons.**

The Serpent is the Dragon, Devil, Satan. He wants to be worshiped like GOD. He is corrupting, beguiling, subtle, fiery, sharp, poisoning, piercing, crooked. He is crafty, cheating, smart, deceiving, cunning, seducing, charming, slandering.

The worship of snakes (serpents) is found in many religions because the snakes represent Satan and his characteristics. There are evil spirits of snakes such as leviathan and other names of those serpents worshiped.

SECTION 16 – DELIVERANCE AMONG AFRICAN-AMERICANS

Ministering Deliverance Within The Context Of The African-American Experience
by Dr. Mary Thomas Oliver

These are some comments for African-American people:

1. They hold onto secrets and the dark side of life. They are tied-up in emotions. **They need to put the emotions on the table and deal with the issues, hurts, fears and anger.**
2. They seek approval but reject it out of fear of the wrong motives of others. The way they treat each other is the way they treat God. When they are overloaded, they cannot stay connected to God. They pull back from God and walk away.
3. The Church is not healthy and not dealing with their own issues. The inward child spirit (boy / girl) gets in the way. Fear is tied to childhood. They are kicking at the pricks.
4. There has been a raw hatred of the race in America. They have become prejudiced and bitter. Those who are older have seen the physical or emotional lynching of people and careers. They hate self because of color. There is a light / dark skin issue. The ceiling to God has become brass and the earth has become iron. Sometimes when they are side by side with a white, the white is favored in housing, check-out counter, etc.
5. They hate themselves but won't admit it. They will change their face and hair to look more white. They feel racist but must deal with it as a Christian. **Slavery has brought a curse on them.** They were beaten into submission. It was planned, perpetuated and thought biblical by whites. **The curse must be broken so that the earth yields its fruits, and they have favor with God and man.**
6. Preachers dispel the myth as head over the body as being prosperous and well thought of. People take care of expenses of family, come to him, drive a nice car, and still have spirits over them. They are bought a car and several suits with Anniversary Week for the pastors. They may have more than one wife and several families even in the same church; one would be legal with the other common law.
7. In slavery, black preachers were given free reign on the plantation with the women who were encouraged to believe in God. He could go from house to house which was expected. He was fed and lay with the women. **These spiritual curses must be broken.**
8. They could be sold to another plantation and start a new family. Children were considered promise seeds to work on the plantation. Black males still do that today and may have many children. This is African culture when man is not the husband of one wife.
9. The Devil needs to be exposed. It doesn't have to be like this. People are blind to the light of God. They must learn what the Scriptures say about them. This is a carry over from slavery and is passed down the generations.
10. Churches need to change and take the lead with a strong voice. There needs to be teaching of the truth where God will be allowed to act. God's anointing will flow with the answers. **Chains and bondage can be broken.**
11. We can setup an operating room and recovery room for deliverance patients. **They have to break the demonic patterns handed down through the generations.** They may need to be filled with The Holy Spirit.
12. No father at home brings rejection. They need the love of The Father God to be approved and accepted.

13. The altar should be open during the service and The Holy Spirit allowed freedom to act. **Imputation and anointing of The Father's love needs to be ministered.**

SECTION 17 - AFRICAN AMERICAN DEMONS
(Ministering Deliverance Within The Context Of The African American Experience)

CONTENTS
1. SINS / CURSES / DEMONS
2. LISTS OF DEMONS
3. SEX
4. INFIRMITY
5. DEATH
6. RELIGION
7. ADDICTIONS
8. SLAVERY
9. BLACK INTERACTION
10. OCCULT
11. BLACK
12. DEMONIC TONGUES
13. MATRIARCHAL

SINS / CURSES / DEMONS

Deuteronomy 27 and 28
Leviticus 26:40

LISTS OF DEMONS

evil soul ties, sins of ancestors, **false self-respect, power, dignity and confidence,** word curses, desire for ungodly power and control, lack of family commitment or commitment to relationships, failure to thrive, forced submissiveness, loss of sons, blind justice, unworthiness, son of Belial, lack of peace, drive by killings, prison bars, slave labor, prejudice, racism, divorce, misplaced and misguided desires, drug sales, poor responsibility and accountability, emotional hurricane, deep sorrow, souls for sale, false prosperity, lack of trust, betrayal, invisibility, pretty children, gold dust, tradition, gambling spirit, divorce, broken marriages, families in rebellion, intimidation, unsaved children and teenagers, loneliness, rejection from the main steam culture, rejection from our spouses, wicked thoughts, stealing other's reputations, coveting, slander, gossip, maliciousness, unholy affections. hurt, sorrow, racist, ungodliness, oppression, temper outburst, refusal behaviors, disgust, failure, beating, lynching, abandonment, loneliness, self-destruction, multiple personalities, double mindedness, schizophrenia, disassociation, pride (Leviathan, strength in his neck), lack of ability to give or receive love, animal spirits, aggression, hollowness, hunger, abduction, kidnap, unbelief, unproductiveness, rage, self-serving spirits, deception, ugly spirit, arrogance, vain imaginations, fits of rage, acrimony, unpleasantness, sullenness, animosity, hostility, provocation, vexation, grief, sorrow, upheaval, insurgence, mutiny, revolution, contentiousness, disputing, stubborn-headed, rebellious attitude against God, defiance, accepts no correction, provoking rejection, stiff-nakedness, overthrowing, destructive, convulsive, resistive, interfering, friction withstanding, repulsiveness, aggression, daring, scornfulness, confusion, division, ridicule, tension, hurt, insults, frustration, disgust, insecurity, difficulty learning, discord, selfishness, doubt, inability to achieve, fake sickness, hypochondriacs, domination

SEX
Rape, birthing illegitimate children, teen pregnancy, prostitution, men sharing, women sharing, low morals, lust not love, barrenness, bastard, flirting, sexual sin, abortions, sexual abuse of children, perversion, homosexuality, seduction, fornication, abuse and rape of women, power in the penis (Behemoth, strength in his loins), sexual promiscuity, adultery, fornication, incest, lust, sodomy, pornography, lesbianism, sex toys, oral sex, anal sex, bestiality

INFIRMITY
Infirmity, high blood pressure, heart disease, arthritis, lupus, cancer, stroke, hardening of arteries, mental illness, worry, pandemonium, anxiety, pharmakeia

DEATH
Death, destruction, Abaddon, Apollyon, suicide, abortion, murder and other crimes, death sentence, early death

RELIGION
False doctrine, abuse of scripture, **false prophesy, wealth or prosperity,** spiritual status, false prestige, preacher's whoop / squall, smooth talking, power of persuasion, domination, manipulation and control, straddling the fence, charmer, spiritual ambitious, lack of accountability, compromise, cover-up, attitude of superiority, verbal and physical abuse, spiritual weakness, vain arguments, profane fictions, abuse of titles, silly myths, irreverent babble, Godless chatter, demonic intercessory prayers, Rastafarianism, village shrine rituals, worship and open relationship with the dead, Orisa Worship (Yoruba), Voodoo (Vodun), ancestor reverence and worship, Religion (magic and healing), spiritualism, witchcraft, nature worship, incense burning, psychic prayers, spirit possession, abuse by men of the cloth, idolatry, Islam, church splits

ADDICTIONS
Addictions (drugs, cigarettes, alcohol, prescription drugs, gambling, excessive spending), self-destruction through use of substances to hide pain, obesity (overweight, love for food, gluttony, overeating, I'm Fat spirit)

SLAVERY
Slavery, spirits of fear, distrust, envy, murder, control, physical abuse, frozen psychic, demonic independence, mental weakness, lynching spirit, vigilante spirit and related spirits.

BLACK INTERACTION
Spirits of distrust, meanness, spitefulness, physical abuse, unfaithfulness, control, disobedience, adultery, fornication, drug addiction, alcoholism, murder, hate, horoscopes, Eastern Star, Islam, hypocrisy and Masonry.

Occult
Roots, Dr. Buzzard, oils (potions, powders, incense), dream books, numerology and other forms of divination, **black, white and candle magic,** dreams, incantation, superstition, occult, herbal

medicine, divination, sorcery, mediumship, necromancy, kinship and royal rituals, ancestral intervention, reincarnation

Black
Down playing or hatred of African features (hair, nose, mouth, skin color), black hatred, hatred for whites, darkie, blackie, black pride, African pride, unlawful transfer of property belonging to blacks, lack of inheritance, poverty

Demonic tongues
Tongue of strange woman and of the serpent, viper's, flattering, smooth, slandering, deceitful, sharp, proud, lying, false, backbiting, stammering, crafty, confused, striving, devises mischief, full of adder's poison, froward, naughty, perverse, evil fire, double, **full of trouble, sin, mischief and iniquity**

Matriarchal
Matriarchal hierarchy due to absence of men in spirit and/or body, matriarchal headed homes, absent fathers, improper family structure, improper male / female relationships, improper alignment, jezebel and ahab spirits

SECTION 18 - STRONGHOLDS IN AFRICAN-AMERICAN FAMILIES

CONTENTS
PREFACE
RELATIONSHIPS
MORALITY AND CHARACTER
RELIGION
    Prayer
    Deliverance
RELIGIOUS SPIRITS
    Control Spirits
    False Spirits
    Witchcraft And Voodoo Spirits
LIST OF DEMONS
    Various Demons
    Sex
    Infirmity
    Death
    Religion
    Addictions
    Slavery
    Black Interaction
    Occult
    Black
    Demonic Tongues
    Matriarchal
REFERENCES

PREFACE
These are characteristics of African Americans. Do you recognize these characteristics?

RELATIONSHIPS
Black Men: You can't trust black women. Black women are mean, spiteful, and they use you. Women are only good for having babies and cooking. You have to slap a woman around every now and then. You have to love them and leave them. **Black Women:** all black men are dogs. Women must take charge and never let a man control them. I can't live without this man. He beats me, but he's a good man. **Black Youth:** My parents don't deserve obedience.

MORALITY AND CHARACTER
Black Men: It's all right to have more than one woman. Drugs and alcohol are not that bad. The only thing that is important is what you do for yourself.
Black Women: You've got to sleep with a man in order to get him.

Black Youth: Everybody else is doing it and so can I. I will do whatever I want. I will hurt others before I hurt myself. I have to do whatever to look cool to my friends and I have to have sex to be accepted by my homeys.

RELIGION

Black Men: I am God. The Bible is the white man's religion. Islam is the black man's religion and the Masons are a good thing.

Black Women: Following my horoscope is all right to engage in and to use to find a mate. Eastern Star is a good thing. Islam is the black man's religion. The church is full of hypocrites. Christianity is a crutch for weak black folks. The Masons are a good thing. I go to church, but I need some stuff from the occult shop too.

Black Youth: There is no God.

Prayer

I forgive all black men, black women and black youth for the way they have treated me. Forgive me for the way I have treated them. In Jesus Name I pray. Amen.

Deliverance

I command the spirits of distrust, meanness, spitefulness, physical abuse, unfaithfulness, control, disobedience, adultery, fornication, drug addiction, alcoholism, murder, hate, horoscopes, Eastern Star, Islam, hypocrisy, and Masonry to manifest and leave me in the Name of Jesus Christ.

RELIGIOUS SPIRITS
Control Spirits

Control By The Church, Control Spirits Of The Bishop Or Preacher, Spirits In Preachers Using Voodoo In Their Ministry To Control People, Loosing Those Who You Worked Voodoo On In The Past, Evil Soul Ties With The Bishop Or Preacher.

False Spirits

False Praise, False Worship, False Holy Dance, False Shouting Spirits, False Dancing In The Spirit, False Voodoo Tongues, False Prophecy, False Baptism Of Fire, False Visions And Dreams, False Voices Calling Themselves God, False Preaching Spirits.

Witchcraft And Voodoo Spirits

Voodoo Spirits, Voodoo Dancing, Jerking Spirits, Shaking Spirits, Quivering Spirits, Spirits That Cause The Body To Twitch, Rocking Backward And Forward Spirits During Preaching And Worship, Spirits That Make The Eyes Roll Back In The Head During Praise, Burning In The Stomach Called The Holy Ghost, Fire Walking Spirits, Veil Over The Eyes Spirit, Spirits Of Divination

LIST OF DEMONS

Deuteronomy 27 and 28
Leviticus 26:40

Various Demons
Evil soul ties, sins of ancestors; **false self-respect, power, dignity and confidence**; word curses, desire for ungodly power and control, lack of family commitment or commitment to relationships, failure to thrive, forced submissiveness, loss of sons, blind justice, unworthiness, son of Belial, lack of peace, drive by killings, prison bars, slave labor, prejudice, racism, divorce, misplaced and misguided desires, drug sales, poor responsibility and accountability, emotional hurricane, deep sorrow, souls for sale, false prosperity, lack of trust, betrayal, invisibility, pretty children, gold dust, tradition, gambling spirit, divorce, broken marriages, families in rebellion, intimidation, unsaved children and teenagers, loneliness, rejection from the main steam culture, rejection from our spouses, wicked thoughts, stealing other's reputations, coveting, slander, gossip, maliciousness, unholy affections. hurt, sorrow, racist, ungodliness, oppression, temper outburst, refusal behaviors, disgust, failure, beating, lynching, abandonment, loneliness, self-destruction, multiple personalities, double mindedness, schizophrenia, disassociation, pride (Leviathan, strength in his neck), lack of ability to give or receive love, animal spirits, aggression, hollowness, hunger, abduction, kidnap, unbelief, unproductiveness, rage, self-serving spirits, deception, ugly spirit, arrogance, vain imaginations, fits of rage, acrimony, unpleasantness, sullenness, animosity, hostility, provocation, vexation, grief, sorrow, upheaval, insurgence, mutiny, revolution, contentiousness, disputing, stubborn-headed, rebellious attitude against God, defiance, accepts no correction, provoking rejection, stiff-nakedness, overthrowing, destructive, convulsive, resistive, interfering, friction withstanding, repulsiveness, aggression, daring, scornfulness, confusion, division, ridicule, tension, hurt, insults, frustration, disgust, insecurity, difficulty learning, discord, selfishness, doubt, inability to achieve, fake sickness, hypochondriacs, domination

Sex
Rape, birthing illegitimate children, teen pregnancy, prostitution, men sharing, women sharing, low morals, lust not love, barrenness, bastard, flirting, sexual sin, abortions, sexual abuse of children, perversion, homosexuality, seduction, fornication, abuse and rape of women, power in the penis (Behemoth, strength in his loins), sexual promiscuity, adultery, fornication, incest, lust, sodomy, pornography, lesbianism, sex toys, oral sex, anal sex, bestiality

Infirmity
Infirmity, high blood pressure, heart disease, arthritis, lupus, cancer, stroke, hardening of arteries, mental illness, worry, pandemonium, anxiety, pharmakeia

Death
Death, destruction, Abaddon, Apollyon, suicide, abortion, murder and other crimes, death sentence, early death

Religion
False doctrine, abuse of scripture; **false prophesy, wealth or prosperity**; spiritual status, false prestige, preacher's whoop / squall, smooth talking, power of persuasion, domination, manipulation and control, straddling the fence, charmer, spiritual ambitious, lack of accountability, compromise, cover-up, attitude of superiority, verbal and physical abuse, spiritual weakness, vain arguments, profane fictions, abuse of titles, silly myths, irreverent babble, Godless chatter, demonic intercessory prayers, Rastafarianism, village shrine rituals, worship and

open relationship with the dead, Orisa Worship (Yoruba), Voodoo (Vodun), ancestor reverence and worship, Religion (magic and healing), spiritualism, witchcraft, nature worship, incense burning, psychic prayers, spirit possession, abuse by men of the cloth, idolatry, Islam, church splits

Addictions

Addictions (drugs, cigarettes, alcohol, prescription drugs, gambling, excessive spending), self-destruction through use of substances to hide pain, obesity (overweight, love for food, gluttony, overeating, I'm Fat spirit)

Slavery

Slavery, spirits of fear, distrust, envy, murder, control, physical abuse, frozen psychic, demonic independence, mental weakness, lynching spirit, vigilante spirit and related spirits.

Black Interaction

Spirits of distrust, meanness, spitefulness, physical abuse, unfaithfulness, control, disobedience, adultery, fornication, drug addiction, alcoholism, murder, hate, horoscopes, Eastern Star, Islam, hypocrisy and Masonry.

Occult

Roots, Dr. Buzzard, oils (potions, powders, incense), dream books, numerology and other forms of divination, **black, white and candle magic,** dreams, incantation, superstition, occult, Herbal Medicine, divination, sorcery, mediumship, necromancy, kinship and royal rituals, ancestral intervention, reincarnation

Black

Down playing or hatred of African features (hair, nose, mouth, skin color), black hatred, hatred for Whites, darkie, blackie, Black pride, African pride, unlawful transfer of property belonging to Blacks, lack of inheritance, poverty

Demonic Tongues

Tongue of strange woman and of the serpent, viper's, flattering, smooth, slandering, deceitful, sharp, proud, lying, false, backbiting, stammering, crafty, confused, striving, devises mischief, full of adder's poison, froward, naughty, perverse, evil fire, double, **full of trouble, sin, mischief and iniquity**

Matriarchal

Matriarchal hierarchy due to absence of men in spirit and/or body, matriarchal headed homes, absent fathers, improper family structure, improper male / female relationships, improper alignment, Jezebel and Ahab spirits

REFERENCES

I recommend that you obtain these books:
Breaking the Curse off Black America by Willie F. Wooten, Lumen-us Publications, Richton Park, IL

Ministering Deliverance Within The Context Of The African American Experience and **Imagination: Who Can Know The Subtle Deceit?** and **Little Boy / Little Girl - The Lust for Approval Spirit** by Mary L. Thomas-Oliver, A Message of Hope Ministries, Brooksville, FL

Breaking Strong Holds in the African-American Family - Strategies for Spiritual Warfare by Clarence Walker, Zondervan Publishing House, Grand Rapids, MI

SECTION 19 - AMERICAN INDIAN CURSES

CONTENTS
1. SCRIPTURES
2. AMERICA IS A MELTING POT
3. EARLINE'S TESTIMONY ABOUT HER HEART CONDITION
    1. Earline
    2. Gene
4. INDIAN CURSES
5. DELIVERANCE OF AN EAGLE SCOUT
6. PRAYER
7. LIST OF DEMONS
8. REFERENCES

SCRIPTURES

Exodus 20	**Sins of Ancestors (Earline's Revelation)**
Exodus 20:3-5	**No other Gods (Idolatry or Idol Worship)**
Leviticus 26:40-41	**Sins of Ancestors (Earline's Revelation)**
Deut. 7:25-26	Graven Images - Abominations
Joshua Ch. 7	Sin of Achan and Accursed Things
II Kings 21:2	Abominations
II Chron. 28:3	Burned Incense and Children
II Chron. 33:2 & 9	Abominations
II Chron. 36:14	Abominations of Heathen
Ezra 6:21	Separated from Heathen
Job 30:3-8	Demons Roam in Wilderness
Psalm 135:15	Idols are Silver and Gold
Jer. 10:2	Signs of Heathen
Ezek. 11:2	Men that Give Wicked Counsel
Ezekiel 18	**Sins of Ancestors (Earline's Revelation)**
Ezek. 20:9 & 14	Not polluted before Heathen
Acts 19:19	Curious Arts and Books
Eph. 5:11-17	Unfruitful works of Darkness

AMERICA IS A MELTING POT

I am Scotch, Irish, English and Welch. This makes me a person of mixed races. How many of you have Indian ancestry? How many of you don't know? Earline found out that there are few pure-blooded American Indians.

EARLINE'S TESTIMONY ABOUT HER HEART CONDITION
Earline

I had a heart condition which was unusual. It never occurred with regularity or under any specific condition. Earline had Cherokee Indian ancestors on both sides of her family.

God gave me a vision of an Indian Shaman or Witch Doctor at an elevated funeral pyre which was burning dead bodies. He was chanting and waving, and saying on the descendents and descendents. This was supposed to be a blessing, but in actuality was a curse, because many Indians worship demons. This was a curse that came down on my family causing heart problems.

Gene

This is a sign of demonic symptoms of disease brought about by a curse. It doesn't follow the medical guidelines. All they can say is that it is inherited.

Earline

While taking a tread mill test, I experienced tremendous pain in the chest, arms and neck. I was examined by a **heart specialist** in Minneapolis who told me that my heart was good but he had written **death by heart attack** on many people's certificates like myself. (These were people who really didn't have anything wrong with their hearts physically but had a curse spiritually.)

Gene

These were people who didn't really have anything wrong with their hearts physically but had a spiritual root to the disease. The prayer of faith will not heal a disease that has a spiritual root that must be dealt with as sin to be confessed. Then the curse can be broken and the person prayed for to be healed.

God is beginning to show the Christian world spiritual roots of various diseases. Pastor Henry Wright of Molena, Georgia is a pioneer in this area. Also Art Mathias who is in Anchorage, Alaska.

Earline

A year or so after my dad's death, I found my heart acting up again. Sometimes one to five years would elapse between seizures. I began to ask God to show me why my brothers, dad, dad's brothers and his dad had heart problems.

God showed me Exodus 20 and Ezekiel 18. He told me to repent for my ancestors and myself for the sin of idol worship in Leviticus 26:40-41. The curse of idol worship follows the blood line down to the descendants. I did these things and have been free from these attacks for over twenty years. I was only the second generation from previous generations of Indians that sinned before God.

Gene

You have to forgive your ancestors and ask for forgiveness for yourself. Earline took her older brother, Clyde, through breaking the curse and he is still alive after a heart attack.

Exodus 20 lists the Ten Commandments which are still applicable today. The scriptures about worshipping other Gods are verses 3, 4 and 5. This outlines the curse for idol worship which lasts three or four generations according to God's purposes. (Does anybody know why God curses some sins for three generations and some sins for four generations?)

Ezekiel 18 shows the equity of God's dealings with us. The sin of idol worship is defined as eating upon the mountains (in the groves), lifting up the eyes to the idols (worship), and not walking in God's statutes and judgments (disobedience).

This was a **revelation of the sins of the ancestors** that God gave Earline through prayer about why her family was plagued by heart attack and death by heart attack. This was primarily the men that were attacked but even Earline, a woman, was attacked. The revelation was the effect of the sins of the ancestors in her family coming through the Indians to cause heart problems and early death. The sin was disobeying the Ten Commandments of having no other Gods before you, which is idol worship, that the Indians committed. Up to that time, we had never heard about the sins of the ancestors. As you look at the list of demons at the end of the lesson, you can identify idol worship; use this list in mass deliverance.

Earline had Cherokee Indian ancestry coming through her father and mother. We were raised in and around Chattanooga, Tennessee which was not far from Cherokee, North Carolina which had a demonic draw upon Earline. We were drawn to make a pilgrimage to the Smokey Mountains every year although we did not make it every year. In the fall, Earline would long to go to the mountains. After Earline was delivered from Indian spirits, she did not have that draw to go to the Smokey Mountains.

When you are a person of mixed races, you inherit the curses coming down through the different races, languages, customs, religions and nationalities. If you have Indian ancestry and are Caucasian, you receive the curses from the Indians and the Caucasians.

The curse would come from those ancestors that had sinned. This means that you can be cursed for ten generations (2046 ancestors) from both sides of your family.

Which of your ancestors didn't sin or that you know didn't sin? It is a good assumption that you have the curse of incest and the curse of the bastard on you. It could come from any of 2046 ancestors back to the tenth generation that sinned assuming it has not been properly broken. You will see the sin repeating itself generation after generation such as bastard after bastard.

We worked with one Indian woman who was a Christian. She had a hard time getting free of Indian curses and demons brought upon her by her ancestral lineage and sexual abuse. She was cursed by being an Indian and by incest which is very hard on a woman being abused by her blood relatives.

INDIAN CURSES (EXCERPTS)

We need to become aware of demonic activity rooted in Indian curses. The American Indian tribes were demon worshippers. When the white man arrived, he did many horrible things to the natives and the Indians retaliated by cursing the land from one end to the other, wherever they went.

Many today have Indian blood because of intermarriage, rape and immorality, and this can bring inherited family curses. So many times in deliverance, we uncover previously unsuspected grounds for attack and harassment coming through these channels.

Win Worley, who I believe was the most-anointed deliverance minister, tangled with a Comanche Indian spirit in a woman. A blue-eyed blonde with Comanche heritage! As the demon manifested and I demanded his name, he answered **Thunderbird!** And what do you do? I asked. **Well, what do you think I do? Stupid! I thunder...I cause commotion. But she won't do it. She is no fun, she just won't do it at all. We haven't given up and are still working on it, but she won't let us do anything.** He then called her some obscenities as we closed in and forced him to go and thunder some other place.

Immediately another Indian spirit manifested. Haughtily he announced he was Firebird. **I strut, I plan, but she's no fun. This stupid woman! I tell her 'paint your face, fix yourself up' but she just won't do it. She likes to be clean and neat. How sickening! I want her to paint her face and eyes like a harlot, but she won't do it.** His frustration over this has ceased for he has gone where it is very dry (Job 30:3-8).

DELIVERANCE OF AN EAGLE SCOUT (EXCERPTS)

Excellent testimony - applies to Boy Scouts, Girl Scouts and forms of scouting. This testimony could be similar to the bondage received from any organization that you give allegiance to that is not of the Lord or has practices that are not Godly. What ungodly organizations are you giving allegiance to?

These three years of learning and games were drawn directly from an Indian background. We were taught about the American Indians. We even had a yell we screamed as a unit: **Akeyla, we will do our best!** Now I believe that **Akeyla** was some **Indian spirit**, possibly a **sun God**. Through scouting I was introduced to **horoscopes**. At the end of my Cub Scouting career, I danced my first Indian dance.

In the scouts there was much tedious work to be done, including lots of memorization, scout oaths, law, etc. We moved to a new house and more and more I became involved in scouting until soon it was absorbing most of my spare time.

As a Cub Scout summer camp staffer, scouting became my goal. The following summer I worked as a staffer at a regular Boy Scout camp and became an Eagle Scout.

The Order of the Arrow is an organization within scouting which takes scouting from regular troops, elected by their fellow troopers. In the ceremony, we symbolically mixed blood, took a log off of a brother's shoulder and put it on our own; symbolically taking their burdens upon us.

You were given a real **Indian name**, actually becoming an Indian. The Order of the Arrow deals with many authentic **ceremonies and dances from Indian demon worship and dancing before evil spirits.** Be careful what you call yourself.

As Guard of the Lodge in the ceremonies that summer, I used my Indian name, and for seven weeks we dressed in authentic Indian costumes. As the spiritual leader per se, of the ceremonies in which I was involved, I moved deeper and deeper into heathenism and sin.

Shortly after this I was baptized in the Holy Spirit, but no one warned me that much I was involved with was wrong. Everything done in scouting is designed to build up the individual in the soulish realm. One of the big points stressed is **self-reliance,** rather than reliance on God as Scripture teaches.

Although scouting did much for me and taught me good things I missed at home and in the classroom, now I realize that it was not without penalty. I had to break very strong, ungodly **soul ties** with my camp director, a scouting professional whom I **idolized.** For example, the main group sponsoring scout troops is the churches, although scouts teach many unscriptural principles.

The number one supporter of the scouts is the Roman Catholic Church. To those saved and Spirit-filled, scouting continues to control and interferes with spiritual growth.

The next fall, as a growing baby Christian, I began to pray and stand on faith for things. It was my senior year in high school. Because I was now very active in sports and scouting, there was no free time to pray or read the Bible.

Help came from an adopted **medicine man,** not a natural Indian by birth, but nevertheless he possessed an unholy power, witchcraft, of which he was unaware. I did recognize what was happening because I had learned some truth. He introduced this ungodly control into the ceremonies I was directing.

This man did Indian dances at the camp and cast curses at us: staff, children, parents on visitor's night, and fathers who stayed with the boys. As Chief of the Lodge and Chief of the Ceremony, I held control. This satisfied a **witchcraft-oriented control** in my life which craved dominance.

I wanted it to be a witness for Him, but He cannot bless what is already cursed in His Word. Some Scripture that I found which applies to my experiences and bears on the abominations of the heathen are: Ephesians 5:6-17; II Kings 21:2; II Chronicles 28:3; 33:2,9; 36:14; Ezra 6:21. **Ye should know that I am the Lord for ye have not walked in my statutes, neither executed my judgments, but have done after the manners of the heathen that are around about you** (Ezekiel 11:12). This is what I had done. Through Ezekiel 20:9, 14 and Psalm 135:15, God spoke to me concerning the many scouting awards I received and the many things which I had made idols in my life.

The idols of the heathen were silver and gold, the work of the man's hands. Indians were great sky watchers, and much of their activity and life was dictated by studying the stars. **Thus saith the Lord, learn not the ways of the heathen, and be not dismayed at the signs of heaven, for the heathen are dismayed at them** (Jeremiah 10:2).

It was real struggle to praise, pray and read the Word. I grew weary of the constant spiritual battles and pressures but the Lord sustained and kept developing me spiritually in spite of the obstacles.

One deliverance uncovered outer layers of **pride, hatred** and many other things which had come through the **Boy Scout spirits.** There was a host of **Indian spirits,** a stronghold of **Indian lore,** and **Indian witchcraft,** tied in with **Indian chants and dances.**

I had two Indian counselors, Sitting Bull and Geronimo, who filled me with **Rebellion, Anger** and **Resentment** toward authority. It was discerned that I had an Indian chief's headdress at home which hindered my deliverance. This was a demonic stronghold and constituted legal grounds for them to stay. They bound up the spirits so I could go home and destroy the remaining artifacts and other scouting treasures that I had saved. These powerful soul ties had such a control over me and were so much a part of me that this was extremely difficult.

As I began to unpack, I began to realize just how much time scouting had taken in my life. When I began to burn my scout treasures, it produced some immediate deliverance. Although I had already renounced scouting and the **Order of the Arrow,** so long as I clung to my mementos there was still bondage.

The Lord gave me Scriptures to encourage me: **The graven images of their Gods shall ye burn with fire; thou shalt not desire the silver or gold that is on them nor take it unto thee, lest thou be snared therein for it is an abomination into thine house, lest thou be a cursed thing like it but thou shalt utterly detest it and thou shalt utterly abhor it for it is a cursed thing** (Deuteronomy 7:25-26; Exodus 20:3; Joshua 7). To me this meant I was not even to save the real gold or silver from the medals and rings but had to destroy them completely. **Many of them also which used curious arts brought their books together and burned them before all men and they counted the price of them and found it fifty thousand pieces of silver, so mightily grew the Word of God and prevailed** (Acts 19:19).

I had to do away with these **idols and curious arts** involving the witchcraft of Indian lore. As I was being freed, I began to wonder what part the Illuminati played in the Boy Scouts of America and how they managed to use the organization to further their destructive conspiracy. From my experience, I believed it has much to do with the control and programming of youth, much as Hitler trained German young people, taking them away from their families.

Immediately following the fire, I noticed I could pray more easily and effectively. I was now able to receive much more deliverance because I had broken the ties with **scouting,** destroying legal grounds for them to stay. **Astrology** was cast out. He had come in through studies for merit badges and the demon bragged that Lucifer was the bright and shining star. Evil soul ties with the bright and shining star had to be broken. Astrology said, **That stupid idiot burned all that stuff! Why did he do that? Why did he choose that? He broke all the holds we had when he destroyed it all.** (There are **seven spirits of Astrology.**) You will receive a measure of freedom when you destroy cursed objects.

When **Indian witchcraft** came up, I began to see Indian faces and saw the face of the **Indian medicine man** who had painted us at camp. His face was running around in my mind, tormenting me, and we cast out his name and his spirit. Next were cast out spirits of **Akeyla, Matoula** (the medicine man I played), **War Whoops,** and **Indian Folk Lore.**

I had renounced the legend I learned from the **Lenelanapa,** the Indian tribe from which the ritual came. The spirit of Lenelanapa (real men) was thrown out. There was a spirit and curse of **Baby Pow** and **Baby Pow Reincarnation.** Baby Pow claimed to be the founder of scouting and this spirit told us that scouting takes the boys from their mothers.

There were many **dance spirits** including **Rain Dance** and **Hoop Dance. Astrology** or **Indian Lore** Merit badges stress the golden rule in scouting, stating that the principle is found in ten major world religions today.

However, in practice they do not warn about the God of this world, and they actually promote other religions as well as Christianity. The **scout spirit** is mentioned frequently and I believe there is an evil spirit driving this movement.

Candles are featured in their ceremonies and they teach scouts can become a candle in the dark. This is a parody of what Jesus taught about being lights in the world.

I learned much **magic** as a Cub Scout and a magic award to be earned got me started into a study of magic. Scouts are absolutely nonsectarian in their attitude towards religious training.

Leaders are urged to **neglect none of the boys, for among them somewhere may be the man who will lead the world to everlasting peace**. Certainly this sounds like the Anti-Christ and scouts are programmed to think that a one-man ruler of peace will come.

When I researched the seemingly harmless **Indian rituals** we had used in ceremonies, I learned of their connection with **demon worship.** They were designed to appease the **evil spirits.**

Some were also spectacular and often remarkable ceremonies pertaining to their many **secret societies.** These were similar in many ways to **Odd Fellows, Free Masons** and other lodges, involving **sun worship** and rooting back to **Baal worship.** It was believed that tobacco was popular with the spirits and Gods, and therefore it was often used in ceremonies. In **dances and rituals** the high point of performances came when the chief participant would lose normal control of himself and enter into another state of existence, the realm of his unconscious. Rites in many cases called for personal tortures which summoned a **vision to bring wisdom and power.** How I praise God each day for deliverance from the lies and deceits of the enemy.

PRAYER

I forgive American Indians and my Indian ancestors for witchcraft against the white man, me and my relatives; for deep-hidden-seething anger-bitterness-resentment-hatred of the white man; for cursing the land and people; for eating and drinking flesh and blood; and for worshipping demons. I forgive the white man for rejecting and enslaving them on the reservation. I forgive the war women for the Jezebelic matriarchal rule of the tribe.

I forgive the witch doctors and shamans for cursing the descendents, dedicating them to Satan, and causing physical problems and diseases. I forgive my ancestors.

I ask forgiveness for myself for the sin of idol worship and disobedience as described in Exodus 20, Leviticus 26 and Ezekiel 18. I ask you to forgive me for any sins associated with Indians such as Scouting. I will destroy Indian artifacts, break ungodly soul ties and break ties to Indian organizations.

I break the curses of incest, rape, immorality and the bastard. I break spiritual roots to any diseases brought about by curses. I break American Indian curses on me and my descendents back to when the white man came to America. I do this in The Name of Jesus Christ, Lord, Master and Savior.

I come against spirits that have been renounced and legal rights taken away; I command that they come out with their families and works as their names are called.

LIST OF DEMONS

Alcoholic spirits (especially firewater & whiskey)
Akeyla (Sun God)
Astrology
Anger
Ancestor Gods
Aiy
Anti-Christ
Amulets
BatGod - Jaguar
Buffalo
Buffalo child (Croaton)
Blood thirsty
Curse of firstborn to pass thru the fire
Child sacrifice
Charms (war, health, ward off evil spirits)
Chac (water God)
Drums
Dominance
Dances (owl, charcoal, sun, snake, duck, chicken, horse, fire leaping, fish, alligator, crow, ghost, buffalo, scalp)
Desertion
Elk Spirits
Divorce
Eliminate curse American Indians
Earth Mother

Break curse of loss of prosperity
Blood brothers & sisters (break ties)
Baby Pow
Baby Pow Reincarnation
Baal Worship
Beads (white - peace; purple - war, death or mourning)
BirdGod (Crocodile)
Bitterness
Cannibalism (Ojibway, Medicine Man)
Caribou spirit
Curse on Arrowhead
Curse to cause cutting off
Hopa doll
Indian rituals
Hypnotic trance
Idol worship
Incantation
Indian Astrology spirits (believed to be ruling spirits) when a star comes earth, it is believed to change into demon.)
Indian Art
Indian artifacts
Indian chants
Indian corn
Indian curses
Indian drumbeat (Voodoo worship)
Indian eye
Indian Fireside Humor spirit (Sioux)
Indian folklore

Eagle
Estsanatlehi (old woman who rejuvenates self)
Earth monster Tlalal-tecuhtli
Hiawatha (glandular malfunctions, swelling)
Father sky
Fox spirit (makes a witch pass thru fire)
Fireside dancer
Fear of lack of provision
False prophecy thru money
False Indian prophecy
False tongues
Feathers
Firebird
FireGod (Xiutechli)
Great Buffalo spirit
God of War (Ojibway)
God fouls of the air (Ojibway)
God of the stars (Ojibway)
God of herbs of the earth (Ojibway)
Great Spirit
Great Lodge
Great White Father
God of the harvest
God of death (Aztec) associated with group KISS
Geronimo
God's eye
Great Father
God of hunting (Ojibway)
Greed
Heavy heart
Human sacrifice
Hoop dance
Horoscopes
Hatred
Peyote eating (open to all drug spirits)
Power over life of animals
Power over death of animals (especially wolf) Crow medicine men
Peace piper
Peace pipe worship (Calumet)
Indian Jezebel
Indian Magic (arrowheads, string, gourd rattles, rawhide, roots, twigs, berries beaks of birds, bird wings, pure white pebbles, turquoise, eagles, blackbirds, peace pipe, bones)
Indian magic spirits
Indian Mythology spirits (for youth)
Indian pierced ear spirit
Indian pierced ears in women, men and children
Indian scalp spirit
Indian spirit of bondage
Indian spirit of poverty
Indian spirit of war
Indian Sorcery
Indian witchcraft (ability to turn oneself into a bear, wolf, fox, owl, snake)
Inherited incest
Knives
Ka-du-te-ta (older women who never die)
Kachina doll
Lenelanapa (Indian Macho man)
Longhouse
Maid of the Mist
Masks for dances
Matolu (chief)
Medicine Bag
Medicine Lodge
Medicine Man
Medicine tipis
Mediums
Moloch
Moon worship
Mother earth
Murder
Nakedness
Necromancy (Ojibway & Cherokee)
Order of the Arrow
Spirit of the Sky
Spirit of the Moon
Spirit of Happy Hunting (powerful death spirit)
Spirit of Animals
Spirit of Trees
Spirit of Grass

Poverty
Pow-wow
Prayer to the Dead (Winnebago, Peyote cult)
Pride
Priesthood of the Bow
Rejection
Raccoon spirits
Reincarnation
Raindance
Rebellion
Resentment
Retaliation
Religious spirits (prophets, priests)
Regeneration, green corn dance
Sacrifice to God of the Harvest
Sacrificial pole
Scout Idols
Scout Oaths
Scout Societies
Seances(Croaton)
Serpent swastika
Shamans (medicine man) seer
Sitting Bull
Si-ka-ma-hi-fi (Elder creator spirit, Hidatsa)
Snake dance
Song to the Morning Star (Pawnee)
Sorcery
Sun worship
Sun Dance (all)
Spirit of the Prairie wolf
Spirit of the Sun
Spirit of the Clouds
Spirit of Water
Spirit of Stones
Spirit of Maize
Spirit of Maple Syrup in trees
Spirit of Nature Worship
Spirit Guides
Squash Blossom
Squirrel Spirits
Stag
Stooped shoulder
Superstition
Submission to tribal custom
Sweat lodges & puberty rites
Teepee
Thief
Thunderbird (Eagle) no head, beak full of rows of wolf's teeth, **powerful ruling spirit in American Indians**)
Sisuitl (soul catcher)
Thunder God (Ibeorhum)
Tobacco Spirits (nicotine, cigarettes, cigar)
Totem pole (Spirit of Theclan)
War God
Warpath
War Whoops
Wigwam (Ojibway)
Will of Wisp
Woe from long march (Mohawk), Six Nations
Wolf
Break curses of Half Breed

REFERENCES
Annihilating The Hosts Of Hell, Books I & II by Win Worley

SECTION 20 - ALASKAN NATIVE CURSES

CONTENTS
1. PREFACE
2. SOCIAL ORGANIZATION
    1. Gender Roles
    2. Marriage
3. RELIGIONS
4. BELIEFS
    1. Unangan
    2. Aleut
    3. Koniag Alutiiq
    4. Central Yup'ik
    5. Inupiat
    6. Athabaskan
    7. Tlingit and Haida
5. KNOWLEDGE SPECIALISTS
    1. Shaman Battle
6. SPIRITUAL CEREMONIES AND RITUALS
    1. Menstrual Period
    2. Slaves
7. CEREMONIAL PARAPHERNALIA
8. OBJECTS
9. ADORNMENT
    1. Tattoos
10. WHALING
    1. Hunter's Wife
11. HUNTING AND FISHING
12. WARFARE AND PEACE
13. DWELLINGS
14. BOATS
15. TOTEM POLES
16. MUMMIES
17. HISTORIC CHANGE
18. FUTURE
19. PRAYER
20. LIST OF SPIRITS
21. REFERENCES

PREFACE

Alaska's indigenous people are jointly called **Alaskan Natives** and could be called **Alaskan Indians** or **American Indians**. There are similarities to the Apache and Navajo Indians. Alaskan Indians are more closely related genetically to other American Indians than they are to **Alaskan Eskimos**. This land is the **deeply-revered** home for Native people.

SOCIAL ORGANIZATION

Matrilineal (traced through the female) descent and inheritance characterized Aleut kinship patterns. A fundamental Athabaskan trait based kinship on matrilineal descent; matrilineal halves were know as **Raven and Seagull**.

Patrilineal-related crews conducted **rituals** prior to whaling and walrus hunting and called on **shamans** for assistance. Gambling was a favorite pastime of many Native men.

The captain was a substantial figure, responsible for many activities including the whale hunt, the ceremonies, festivals, **religious rituals** and trading expeditions. In Inupiat **belief and practice,** husband and wife both must carry out their **spiritual and secular responsibilities** so the captain was worthy to receive a whale.

Preferential female infanticide was practiced, but due to the many accidental deaths suffered by males, the number of adult men and women tended to be fairly balanced.

Individuals were born into these totemic corporate groups which traced their origins from **mythical or legendary incidents.** The clans were typically named after an **animal or mythical being.** For example, the Kiksadi, a important clan among the Sitka people, claimed the **frog** as its major symbol or crest. Classes are usually divided into the **nobles or aristocracy, the commoners and the slaves.**

Gender Roles

Among the Alutiiq, **gender roles for men as women and women as men** were both recognized. Despite the cultural emphasis on male hardiness and self-reliance, there was a recognized role in Unangan society for the **male transvestite who dressed and worked as a woman**. They were often considered **experts in healing.**

Marriage

Wealthier males occasionally had several wives and, among the Gwich'in, might use **younger males to sire heirs by their younger wives.** These long-standing relationships could include **short-term exchanges of spouses** as part of the generosity between the two families. Among the Gwich'in, high-status women occasionally had unions to brothers (woman married to several men).

An individual was a member of one side, **Raven and Eagle or Wolf,** and had to obtain a marriage partner from the opposite side; to marry or have sexual relations with a member of one's own side was considered **incestuous.** Marriages, particularly among the nobles, were arranged by the **mother and her brother** for the woman's children.

RELIGIONS

The first foreign religion introduced into Alaska was **Russian Orthodox.** Alaska has been subjected to catholic religious influence. In 1882, Jackson convened a meeting of Christian missionaries from various sects interested in proselytizing in Alaska and through mutual agreement, **different sects were assigned to different areas of Alaska.**

BELIEFS
Unangan

Although little is known of the Unangan belief system, they appear to have conceived of a **creator deity related to the sun** who was instrumental in hunting success and the **reincarnation of souls**. Small **images** of the creator, were carved from ivory and hung from the ceiling beams. The creator, however, had little impact on everyday life which was instead influenced by **two classes of spirits, good and evil.** Animals also had spirits. The most important ones were those of the **whale** and **sea otter.** The Unangan believed in the **reincarnation of souls** which migrated between the earth, a world below and a world above.

Aleut

Aleut men wore a variety of **amulets and charms** that were thought to provide **special powers from the animal spirits** to enhance success in hunting.

Koniag Alutiiq

Koniag Alutiiq cosmology was elaborate consisting of origin accounts involving a **primeval sun-man,** accounts of **spiritual forces,** and numerous oral texts about how the universe functioned and how humans were supposed to behave. Both **good and evil spirits** existed.

Central Yup'ik

Among the Central Yup'ik was a **universal cosmic presence** who coordinated existence and established a basic ordering framework. The first of these is that all living beings have a spiritual essence that is sentient and volitional and human beings **must maintain respectful relations with the animal and organisms** on which they depend. The second principle is that of **reincarnation or cosmological cycling of the spiritual essence, the person of life. Powerful spiritual beings** controlled the recycling of different animal, fish and bird forms and determined where they would go to give themselves to worthy people.

Inupiat

The Inupiat belief system appears to have been based on the principle of **reincarnation and the recycling of spirit forms** from one life to the next. This was true of both the **human and animal worlds. Names of those who had recently died** would be given to newborn infants. **Animal spirits** were seen as critical for only if they were released could the animal be regenerated and return for future human harvest. Consequently a great number of special behaviors were accorded various animals including **offering marine mammals a drink of freshwater, cutting the throats or skull to release the spirit,** and taking care to make maximum use of the products. **Shamans** had a special place in Inupiat society as **curers, and forecasters of weather and future events. Healers** (usually women) expert in the medicinal uses of plants also helped maintain Inupiat health.

Athabaskan

A critical set of beliefs revolved around the **similarities between men and animals** in the distant past. Both have spirits and in the past **they communicated directly with each other.** These ancient relationships had been transformed by the acts and antics of **Raven, a culture hero and trickster** who constantly disrupted the moral order by deception. The **legend cycle,** told in stories to Athabaskan children, is composed of **tales** concerning the activities of **Raven, along with other mythical beings** which exemplify concepts of right and wrong in Athabaskan culture.

Despite the transformations, **important relationships between the spirits of men and animals** continue. Humans must remain respectful through **ritual practices,** such as sexual abstinence and **taboos,** in order to remain in the good graces of the **animal spirits.** Some individuals might obtain **power through a special relationship with the spirit of an animal species. Malevolent spirits** must not be offended. Among the Pacific Athabaskans, the **shaman was an important intermediary with the spirits. Shamans** acted as both **magician and medical practitioner** and could have either a **good or bad reputation. Curing and predicting future events** such as weather and hunting success were important activities of the shaman. Among the upland groups, shamans utilized **scapulimancy,** a method of **divining** the location of game when hunting success was limited.

Tlingit And Haida

The belief system of both the Tlingit and Haida were linked to the **Raven, a supernatural trickster** through whose activities most of the universe's features came to be. Other animals were also important as actors in Tlingit and Haida **myths and legends;** particularly important were bears, the **Thunderbird** and a variety of other **mythical beings and spirits** whose acts influenced human affairs. Tlingits undertook purification and cleansing by immersion in freshwater **to acquire personal guardian spirits** to assist them in daily life. Both cultures had a strong belief in **reincarnation** which was identified by dreams and physical or behavioral similarities of new born children to some recently deceased person. The **shaman** was a **powerful ritualist** in both societies who **acquired spiritual forces** through fasting, abstinence and retreat to nature to assist in **curing, foretelling future events,** and of major importance, **identifying witches** who were damaging other persons. **Shamans,** unlike other Tlingits who were cremated following death, were buried in boxes, and accompanied by **their spiritual materials,** taken to uninhabited forest areas at a distance from villages and camps. Their remains were never bothered out of **respect and fear.**

KNOWLEDGE SPECIALISTS

Among the Alutiiq, **knowledge specialists** were present whose expertise covered different domains such as **medicinal healing, divination, marshaling spiritual forces,** and maintaining social order. Apparently unique among Alaska Natives, Koniag Alutiiq communities had persons known as **wise men** (revered elders who were the **ritual leaders of the winter masked ceremonials.** As bearers of the **cosmological truths,** they were capable of **communicating with the most powerful spirits as well as with the spirits of the animals.** For Koniag Alutiiq, the influence and capabilities were viewed as separate from, superior to and more important than **the shamans.**

Kalaik, both men and women, had **spiritual assistants whose powers they called upon** to predict the outcome of hunts, battles and travels, and to **discern,** and endeavor to alter weather, prevent calamities, and heal certain kinds of sickness. Some sources suggest that certain shamans obtained **powers form evil spirits** and that **bad shamans** used their powers to bring harm to humans. **Shamanic powers** were activated spiritually through unusual clothing, facial painting, special objects, rattles, whistles, song, dance, gestures, and formulaic verbalizations. Another category of **knowledge specialist** was the **medicinal curer** who utilized a diverse array of more physically-based techniques in their healing practices and passed their knowledge on to descendants. Included in the repertoires of these healers were herbs for beverages, foods and poultices, **acupuncture, blood letting,** surgical procedures and bone setting.

Shaman Battle

Shamans were thought to travel great distances to see events in other communities and do battle with other shamans. A challenger traveled to the **spiritually-significant Augustine Island,** an active volcano located in lower Cook Inlet, where he found Abshala. On the island, Abshala was ultimately victorious as his spectacular display of fiery rockets overwhelmed the rival, forcing him to admit defeat and depart.

SPIRITUAL CEREMONIES AND RITUALS

Fathers, supported by their kinsmen, were responsible for hosting the feast and distributing food and gifts to guests who were invited to witness **the ceremonial transformation of a young man** after a successful sea lion or bear hunt. Central to the religious practices of the Alutiiq were the **masked winter dances** and ritual performances conducted. A primary focus of these activities was to **thank and show respect to spirits controlling the availability and abundance of game.** Presentations included **dramatic appearances and disappearances** from the smoke hole in the ceiling. Through the drum, the heartbeat of the spirit was felt and it joined the heartbeats of all participants in the ceremonies through song and dance. New clothes and equipment were brought out because this was a **festival of renewal, or insuring the continuation of life.** Due to a combination of grieving and **fear of the corpse,** most were cremated but **shamans** would be interred in coffins away from the community.

Menstrual Period

A number of **taboos** were imposed and she was expected to stay away from contact with men and their hunting gear for **fear of polluting it** from the **ritual** associated with a young woman's first menstruation. During the seclusion, she received focused training on her physical transformation, on the **behavioral taboos** and requirements during her menstrual period.

Slaves

Slaves were fairly numerous and were important in both trade and providing labor. They were also important at potlaches when they might be **either killed or released.** The Koniag also held a substantial number of **slaves,** who consisted primarily of women and young people captured in raids or battles. **Slavery** was practiced among a number of Athabaskan groups, but was almost incidental, typically consisting of women or children captured in raids from other groups.

CEREMONIAL PARAPHERNALIA

Wooden masks were used in some dances **to invoke the presence of powerful spirits.** The exquisite quality and rarity of such lamps suggest they may have been used only in rituals. The Koniag used small carved wooden dolls for several purposes. These may have been used in **ceremonial performances** or attached to dance masks.

Among the Koniag and lower Kenai Peninsula Alutiiq, **dances to mollify evil spirits** were a part of the ceremonies. Alutiq **masks were the presence and embodiment of spiritual forces.** One of the most important practices was the bringing out of elaborate masks that embodied **the spirit** who was honored by such representation.

The Yupiit cosmos was inhabited by **many spirits** including those of the deceased. **Spirit poles** were erected by graves to keep the spirits of the dead who wished to be reborn from disrupting the world of the living.

Masks representing **animal and other spirits** were an important part of **religious ceremonies and dances** among the Central Yupiit. Since it was believed that **the seal spirits** would return at that time to the vicinity to witness the ceremony, noise was kept at a minimum in order not to disturb the seal spirits. The **shaman** had a special role for he was to leave the festival and travel to the home of the seals to see if they had been satisfied with the human efforts.

OBJECTS

The Chugach paintings in Prince William Sound are believed to be **ritual art forms** made by whalers to call up **powerful spiritual assistance** for their hunting efforts. Some of the smaller objects include bear's heads and an extraordinary figurine that depicts a **human to bird transformation.** Another type of figure is the **shaman's doll.** Prior to the beginning of the masked ceremonies, the shaman brought out the doll and visited each household where the heads placed marks on the doll indicating what they hoped the **spirits would provide for them** during the upcoming season.

ADORNMENT

Nose pins were worn by men and women. **Flat circular discs** made of wood or ivory were inserted into slits in the area between the lower lip and the chin. Nunivak men wore ivory **labrets** through pierced holes below both ends of the lower lip.

Tattoos

Simple tattoos, usually from short straight lines, were inscribed on the hands and faces. Three parallel straight **tattoo** lines down the lower lip were common among women. Some men and women also had relatively limited **tattoos,** usually single lines encircling the face or crossing the cheeks. Among the Koniag these were utilized by **shamans** and others who participated in **ritual ceremonies.**

WHALING

A very elaborate type of visored headgear was worn by the Koniag whalers that was a symbolic component of their **ritualized hunting transformation into a type of killer whale.** Whalers were **ritual and knowledge specialists** who were viewed with both **awe and horror** by their fellow Alutiiq. Koniag whalers left their villages and went to solitary retreats in caves or secluded coves in April, perhaps a month prior to the arrival of whales, **to ritually transform themselves.** They had to **activate their amulets or talismans through ritual procedures to access their power.**

Perhaps the most unique practice of the Koniag whaler was the **use of rendered human fat in their hunting.** Then he would proceed into the bay and after **vocally calling on his spiritual supporters and the sun** for assistance, would go and harpoon the whale. Once the whale was struck, the whaler would use **song and motion to tow** the whale ashore. At the conclusion of the whaling season, the whaler had to **ritually cleanse and decommission himself.** Only by **transforming himself back to his other human form** would he be able to return to the village and live. Whalers had to go through a similar set of ritual preparations and also were said to use **human fat** to keep struck whales in the bays.

Unangan whaling was a highly ritualized activity for which men and their wives prepared themselves by abstinence and other behaviors to make themselves worthy. The stone harpoon heads were coated with a **magical** poison concocted from the aconite plant. During this time, the hunter who struck the whale secluded himself in his house and pretended to be ill hoping that the whale likewise would become sick and die.

Hunter's Wife

Throughout these preparations and practices, the whaler's wife, who had remained behind in the village, had **a strict set of behaviors** she was to follow including not leaving the house, limiting her movements and keeping her voice down.

Wives observed **many taboos and rituals** to assist their husbands' hunting. These included a broad range of activities such as **cutting skins at certain times,** eating certain foods or **looking in certain directions.** It was thought that if those taboos were broken, then **bad luck** would befall the husband's hunting efforts.

HUNTING AND FISHING

Halibut hooks were carved with **representations of powerful spirits** called upon by the fishermen to assist their efforts. A **strong spirit** was needed to overcome the strength of the halibut. Special clubs were made for dispatching the powerful halibut when brought to the surface where they were **ceremoniously greeted and thanked.** ANCSA also explicitly extinguished all **aboriginal hunting and fishing rights.**

WARFARE AND PEACE

The Koniag were reported by Russian sources to have traditionally **tortured some male captives prior to killing them.** The Koyukon, Gwich'in and Dena'ina were noted for **warfare. Warfare** was a common practice among both Tlingit and Haida. **Feuding,** the perpetuation of multi-generation hostilities between two clan groups, was also well known.

A major mechanism used to restore balance was the **Deer ceremony.** This was a **sacred ritual** involving, among several elements, the exchange of high raking persons from the two clans; their role was to demonstrate the dampening of anger and rise of peaceful feelings.

Within the local group, tensions between men could be controlled through the **song duel.** In this event, a man who felt wronged by another would challenge him to an exchange of **belittling songs.**

DWELLINGS

Steaming provided a combination of cleansing, **spiritual purification,** relaxation and socializing for the people. Finally, the building became the ceremonial structure during the winter festivities, **religious rituals and ceremonies.**

BOATS

Special thanks were given to the tree prior to felling and each morning the craftsman **prayed that his efforts would be well received.**

TOTEM POLES

Mortuary posts were erected in memory of a deceased clan head often having a niche carved in the back for placement of ashes of the deceased. Chief Skowl, a Kaigani Haida, erected a pole with carved images of Russian Orthodox priests **to memorialize his opposition to Christian beliefs.**

MUMMIES

The special importance of **death and the spirit of the deceased** is apparent in the distinctive mummification practices of the Unangan. Mummification was practiced **to preserve the spiritual power which resides in each person.**

These powers could be solicited at a later time by emboldened Unangan hunters who visited the caves and took a bit of flesh from one of the mummies, hoping it would bring assistance in whaling. But this was dangerous and those who sought such power might be subject to **insanity, severe sickness, and early death.**

HISTORIC CHANGE

In the aftermath, Russians began asserting total control over Koniag life, acquiring hostages and requiring males to hunt sea otter, often in distant waters. The Unangan were **violently subjugated** and decimated by disease. Russian Orthodox clerics tried to stop **many abuses** against the Unangan. The priests quickly became critics of **the brutal Russian American Company** practices toward indigenous people and argued for more humane policies. Russian methods had changed by this time with **severe terms of trade** and missionaries replacing outright subjugation. The legacy of the Russian period included smallpox and **venereal disease** that wreaked great havoc throughout the southern coastal regions.

In the 18th century, a violent group of men, driven by the ruthless quest for profits at any cost, descended on the Unangan, and their coming eventually resulted in the destruction of this unique system of cultural adaptations.

The outposts were manned by an **extremely uncouth and rugged breed of soldier** who apparently contributed substantially to the difficulties of the Native groups. One of the results of the military presence was teaching the Tlingit how to **make homebrew.**

Unfortunately, less savory traders brought **liquor** to Native villages, causing major problems. This contact brought new material goods, opportunities for trade and labor, and **diseases** which decimated the north coast in the 1880's. But no Alaska Native groups were able to escape **the ravages of disease.**

FUTURE

There are also significant problems associated with cultural changes such as **alcoholism, drug addiction, heart disease and diabetes** from altered diets, high rate of **fetal alcohol syndrome,** and **serious abuse of women and children.** Alaska Natives are also incarcerated at disproportionate levels and experience **the highest suicide rate in the nation.**

PRAYER

I forgive my ancestors, descendents and others, ask you to forgive me and I forgive myself for worshiping traditions and idols, alcohol and drug abuse, rape, sexual abuse and perversion, murder, self bitterness and hatred, occult, Americans and religions for suppressing religious and cultural practices, having to depend on welfare, reversing gender roles; multiple spouses; **false religions and demonic beliefs, ceremonies, dances and rituals, having demonic paraphernalia, talismans, amulets, charms, spirit poles, objects, adornment and tattoos;** sins of Alaskan Natives, Indians and Eskimos; **Russians, traders, soldiers and others for mistreating my ancestors;** those who brought alcoholism, drug addiction, heart disease, diabetes, fetal alcohol syndrome, serious abuse of women and children, incarceration and suicide upon my people; **being warlike, taking slaves, barbarism, torture and cruelty;** following shamans and wise men; for worshiping and following demons; **tribes, clans and groups for their demonic beliefs;** preferential female infanticide; following myths and legends; **transvestites, adultery, wife swapping and incest;** seeking help from evil spirits; **worshipping animals and their spirits;** reincarnation and ancestor worship; acquiring guardian spirits; seeking forbidden knowledge; demonic healing and divination; worship of nature and earth; **transformation into animals and animals into humans;** fears of death and shamans; mistreating and killing slaves; cutting the flesh; using human fat and mummies; magic and witchcraft; superstition and taboos; **insanity, severe sickness, early death and diseases of Alaska.** I do this in **THE NAME OF JESUS CHRIST: LORD, MASTER AND SAVIOR. We come against spirits that have been renounced and legal rights taken away, and command that they come out with their families and works as their names are called.**

BASIC DELIVERANCE

1. **Prayer**
2. **List of Demons for Basic Deliverance**
   Spirits of Rejection
   Spirits of Bitterness
   Spirits of Rebellion

LIST OF SPIRITS

Rape, sexual abuse, sexual perversion, murder, self bitterness, self hatred, occultism, welfare dependence, reversing gender roles, multiple marriages, **false religions, demonic traditions, beliefs, ceremonies, dances and rituals;** slavery, **having demonic paraphernalia, talismans, amulets, charms, spirit poles, objects, adornment and tattoos;** Alaskan Native, Indian and Eskimo spirits; **alcoholism, drug addiction, heart disease, diabetes, fetal alcohol syndrome, abuse of women and children, incarceration and suicide;** barbarism, torture and cruelty; following shamans and wise men; worshiping demons; **tribe, clan and group spirits;** female infanticide; following myths and legends; **transvestites, adultery, wife swapping and incest;** seeking help from evil spirits; reincarnation and ancestor worship; animism, guardian spirits; seeking forbidden knowledge; demonic healing and divination; worship of nature; **transformation into animals and animals into humans;** fears of death and shamans; cutting of the flesh; using human fat and mummies; magic and witchcraft; superstition and taboos; **insanity, sickness, death and diseases of Alaska.**

REFERENCES

The Native People of Alaska (Traditional Living in a Northern Land) by Steve J. Langdon. This lesson was primarily taken from this book which is especially recommended for study.
Native Peoples of Alaska (A Traveler's Guide To Land, Art, And Culture) by Jan Halliday with Patricia J. Petrivelli and The Alaska Native Heritage Center
The Wolf and the Raven (Totem Poles Of Southeastern Alaska) by Viola E. Garfield and Linn A. Forrest
Alaska Geographic (Russian America), (Inupiaq and Yupik People of Alaska) and **(Native Cultures in Alaska)** Russian America is especially recommended.
Alaska, An American Colony (A New History) by Stephen Haycox

Made in the USA
Las Vegas, NV
10 March 2025